MINDFUL
moments

D1072836

Louise Adams

FEB   2017

Louise Adams is an Australian clinical psychologist who specialises in health and wellbeing. Central to her practice is compassion based mindfulness, which has profoundly improved not only Louise's life but those of her clients. Louise's passion is to help people learn how to treat themselves well through all of life's ups and downs. In addition to running her busy private practice, Louise developed the Treat Yourself Well Online program (www.treatyourselfwell.com.au), which helps people all over the world develop a balanced approach to psychological and physical health. Louise regularly appears on television, radio & print media talking about compassion, mindfulness, health & wellbeing. She also runs training workshops for other health professionals, and with Fiona Willer, APD, has co-authored The Non-Diet Guidebook For Psychologists & Counsellors (2014).

WP

Published by:
Wilkinson Publishing Pty Ltd
ACN 006 042 173
Level 4, 2 Collins St Melbourne, Victoria, Australia 3000
Ph: +61 3 9654 5446
www.wilkinsonpublishing.com.au

International distribution by Pineapple Media Limited
(www.pineapple-media.com)   ISSN 2203-2270

Copyright © 2016

All rights reserved. No part of this publication may be reproduced, stored in a retrieval system or transmitted in any form by any means without the prior permission of the copyright owner. Enquiries should be made to the publisher.

Every effort has been made to ensure that this book is free from error or omissions. However, the Publisher, the Author, the Editor or their respective employees or agents, shall not accept responsibility for injury, loss or damage occasioned to any person acting or refraining from action as a result of material in this book whether or not such injury, loss or damage is in any way due to any negligent act or omission, breach of duty or default on the part of the Publisher, the Author, the Editor, or their respective employees or agents.

The Author, the Publisher, the Editor and their respective employees or agents do not accept any responsibility for the actions of any person - actions which are related in any way to information contained in this book.

National Library of Australia Cataloguing-in-Publication data:

Creator:	Adams, Louise, author.
Title:	Mindful moments / Louise Adams.
ISBN:	9781925265521 (paperback)
Subjects:	Mindfulness (Psychology)
	Awareness.
	Mind and body.
Dewey Number:	158.1
Layout Design:	Tango Media Pty Ltd
Cover Design:	Tango Media Pty Ltd

Photos by agreement with iStock.

CONTENTS

INTRODUCTION

ABOUT ME

Hi, my name is Louise Adams, and I'm a clinical psychologist. I specialise in helping people build a healthier relationship with their minds and bodies.

My university training in clinical psychology gave me the **skills to help people** with a huge variety of life problems. As an evidence-based practitioner, I only use strategies and treatments that scientific research has shown to be effective in helping people out. For the most part, cognitive behavioural therapy (CBT) formed the basis of my approach, because it has an enormous amount of research to show its effectiveness in **getting people well.** Cognitive behavioural therapy involves helping people to identify patterns of thoughts, feelings, and behaviour that are holding them back, and teaching them ways to combat them and make change. Over the years I have treated thousands of people with every kind of trouble you can imagine, mostly using this CBT focus.

Several years ago I came across **mindfulness techniques,** and I was amazed at how this changed the way I worked, and lived. The simple concepts: coming into the present moment, building awareness, learning detachment – were an incredibly powerful addition to my practice. I quickly found that including mindfulness training in my treatment sessions improved the CBT results – people got better much more quickly.

Delving more deeply into mindfulness concepts, I came across the work of Kristen Neff in self-compassion. This was truly transforming: in addition to mindful awareness, self-compassion promoted the idea of **responding to oneself with kindness,** compassion and a desire to soothe. Many of my clients experienced a high degree of shame associated with their psychological problems, and as a result I saw a lot of people judging themselves harshly when they came into sessions. Simple mindful awareness of this didn't help alleviate this shame: they needed something more. Self-compassion was the answer, the solution to this terrible suffering. Once I started to use self-compassion based mindfulness techniques, the change was incredible. Shame vanished and was replaced with **care, concern, and a desire to heal**. People were able to learn this skill relatively easily, and it fundamentally shifted their attitude towards themselves. Both personally and professionally, I have found this practice immensely rewarding.

So what I do is best described as a **compassion-based mindfulness** approach, on top of more traditional CBT strategies to help people get the most out of their lives. A more simple way to put it is 'kindfulness'.

I've taken what I do in my everyday sessions, and put it all here, in the hope that it can be of some benefit to you. I hope you enjoy this book, I hope you enjoy taking things a little deeper and discovering for yourself just how transformative being a little more kindful can be.

WHO HAS TIME FOR THIS?

I'm a human being like everybody else. My life is super busy. I'm raising two young children, by myself. I own my own private psychology practice, so in reality I juggle two jobs – as a clinician,

Self-compassion was the answer, the solution to this terrible suffering.

and also as a business owner. Oh, and a third job now, as a writer!

I champion self-care and compassion based mindfulness practice, but I don't have a lot of time to practice it. When I first trained in mindfulness, the general consensus was that you needed to do **formal meditation practice** for at least twenty minutes a day. While I loved the idea of mindfulness, and was very impressed with the scientific research which was consistently showing phenomenal results, I simply couldn't devote myself to that kind of regime.

Over the years I have developed my own way of incorporating mindful self-compassion practice into my day. It's rarely twenty minute stretches! But I make sure I include what I call '**mindful moments' each day,** and these have helped me through the most difficult times in my life. This practice has brought a richness and an appreciation to my experiences that I truly treasure.

In my work I'm lucky enough to teach my clients how to do the same. My clients are busy people as well. Mindful moments are **easy, fun, and deeply enriching.** The premise of this approach is if you can't find the time to drop into formal mindfulness practice, you can dip your toe in for just a moment, and make it delicious.

The four week program presented in this book gives you a simple, gentle plan to help you include self-compassion and mindfulness in your day to day life. You only need five minutes a day, and what you'll get back will be worth it, I promise you!

WHY COMPASSIONATE MINDFULNESS IS SO AMAZING

I'm an evidence based practitioner, which means that I am trained in scientific thinking. I don't recommend or use techniques that haven't been rigorously researched and found to be effective.

Scientific research on the link between mindfulness practice and improved mental health is now very firmly established. Mindfulness not only helps people to reduce anxiety and depression, it enhances mental well-being. There has been a multitude of research papers on hundreds of topics demonstrating the power of mindfulness practice. Mindfulness training actually **changes how the brain works:** MRI imaging shows that people who do mindfulness training show changes in their gray matter, specifically those involved in learning and memory processes, emotion regulation, self-referential processing, and perspective taking. Every day, more research is discovering how mindfulness training changes the brain's structure.

What I like about it is that mindfulness doesn't just work for people with psychological 'problems'. It also enhances the joy and meaning in the **life of everyday people** who might not be going through particularly challenging psychological issues. Mindfulness isn't just about trying to not be sick, it's about embracing wellness.

The research on compassion-focussed mindfulness is particularly exciting. Although scientific study of self-compassion is fairly new, it's bringing about uniformly positive results. When a self-compassion focus is added to traditional psychological therapy, outcomes are improved and change tends to stick around for longer. People who are highly self-compassionate are more resilient with life's ups and downs, and experience **less anxiety, depression and stress** than people low in self-compassion. People who learn self-compassion become more motivated to use self-care behaviours – to look after themselves well. They are also less afraid of failure, and more likely to keep trying even if they do fail. The skill of self-compassion seems to **'super-charge'** positive change. I've certainly seen the results in my clinical practice, and in my own life.

WHAT MAKES THIS BOOK DIFFERENT?

There are thousands of books written about mindfulness practice. I have found that most books focus on 'surface level', basic mindfulness skills: breathing exercises, being present, seeing things as they are, acceptance. These skills are very important and often life changing: many people report better stress management, more of a **sense of peace,** once they start to use them.

What many books don't address is what to do once you've noticed things about yourself that perhaps you don't like. **Awareness** of the present moment is a tremendously important first step in developing mindfulness skills, but it is only a first step. Once people have achieved mindful awareness, then what?

Perhaps the reason that so many mindfulness books stop at the level of awareness is that meditation experts wrote them rather than behaviour change experts. This is where I come in: **behaviour change** is something psychologists are trained in.

In my clinical practice I use compassion focussed mindfulness techniques in addition to using evidence based techniques to get people to change how they live. This means that my clients not only learn how to increase their awareness and detachment from their thoughts and feelings, but they then learn how to take the next step and start living according to their values.

This is why I wrote this book: to take the practice of compassion based mindfulness a little deeper, to offer people **effective strategies** to change. This book is a combination of compassion based mindfulness training and evidence based psychological strategies to help you to live a more meaningful life. I hope you enjoy reading it as much as I have enjoyed creating it.

Mindfulness isn't just about trying to not be sick, it's about embracing wellness.

CHAPTER ONE:

OUR MAD MINDS:
Why We Need Compassionate Mindfulness

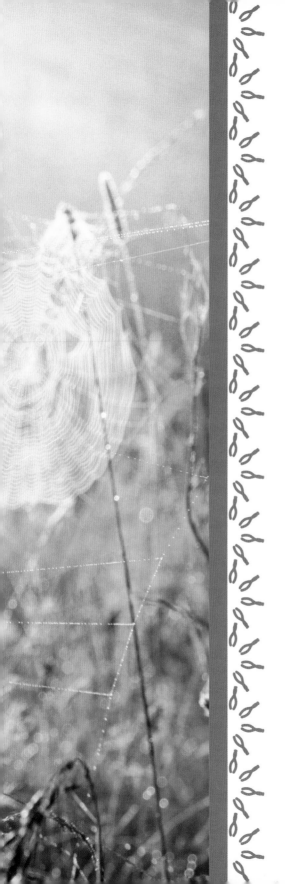

The phrase "going out of your mind" isn't widely regarded as a good idea, but essentially that's the idea with mindfulness. All of us think, all of us talk to ourselves. In psychology this inner voice is called 'self-talk', or the 'thinking mind'. And it never stops. Our minds are **always switched on**. As a result, our minds can be very loud, incessant, relentless places to be.

THINKING IS TIRING

Now don't get me wrong: thinking is an excellent human trait. Our thinking minds give us brilliant ideas, they give us advice on how to solve our problems, they help us remember things to do and keep us **engaged and interested** in the world. But a conversation that never stops can get exhausting. We all know how it feels when we get stuck with a 'talker' at a party – it can quickly become draining and we get the urge to get away from the noise! It's a bit like that with our own minds, the problem is however that we can't physically get away from it. This is one reason that learning -compassionate mindfulness is useful: it can help us to take a break from our busy, mad minds!

WE'RE HARDLY EVER HERE

When we start to listen to our thoughts, it's amazing how much of the time our minds are either in the future – planning what's next, or in the past, going over what went wrong. Being elsewhere is a very common 'default'. In evolutionary terms, having what we call a 'threat-related brain' was extremely useful. It meant that our minds were wired to think about potential problems in the future, and to come up with solutions to them. Going over our mistakes from the past also gave us the opportunity to not make them again, and therefore we flourished as a species.

Our 'threat-primed' brain persists today, and is still a useful resource to identify and correct potential problems.

But the down side of an eternally vigilant brain is that it's difficult to stop and simply be present in the moment. Paying so much attention to the negative also means we can miss the joy, and the wonder, of being alive. This is where mindfulness training can help. By **focusing** more upon the present moment and less on the present or the future, we have more opportunity to enjoy what's actually going on in our lives.

THINKING IS WILDLY INACCURATE

Much of our thinking is 'automatic' – **thoughts just pop up, uninvited.** My client Sylvia, a 35 year old new mum, came to see me because she kept having very frightening thoughts about the

Our inner bully is responsible for a whole host of terrible emotions.

health of her baby. Her thoughts were

(when she checked on her daughter napping) "Oh my God! Is she breathing? She looks dead!"

(Walking up the hallway) "What if I drop her?"

(when the baby was crying) "Something must be wrong! What if it's meningitis?"

Objectively nothing was wrong with the baby, who was healthy at birth and had never even had a cold, but Sylvia's **thinking mind was convinced** that something was dreadfully wrong, or that something would soon go dreadfully wrong. Obviously these thoughts were causing Sylvia enormous distress – because she believed them. And that's the thing with thinking minds – thoughts pop up, and we just believe them – we never pause long enough to consider if what we're telling ourselves is **objectively true, or likely, or helpful.** We just swallow it, hook, line & sinker. And it's this *belief* in our thinking that makes us feel bad.

OUR MINDS ARE MEAN TO US

Not only are our minds noisy, stuck in the future or the past, and full of inaccurate thoughts, they are downright nasty to us. Our self-talk is liberally peppered with judgement.

"You should know better, you idiot!"

"I can't believe what a coward you are!"

"You're pathetic!"

This inner critic is never satisfied, is constantly finding fault and insists that we should do better. Many of my clients admit that they are their own worst enemies and that they would never dream of speaking to another human being the way they speak to themselves.

Once again, we don't ask for this nasty inner voice to show up, it just happens automatically. For many of us being **cruel towards ourselves** is our 'default'. We're effortlessly horrible to ourselves at every turn. Far from having our own back, in life we're much more likely to stab ourselves in it!

Our inner bully is responsible for a whole host of terrible emotions, like guilt, shame, sadness, hopelessness. In our culture we tend to believe that being nasty to ourselves will somehow **'motivate' us to 'be better'.** But the reality couldn't be farther from the truth: we know that harsh self-judgement is strongly related to people 'freezing' and giving up trying to be 'better'. A far more psychologically healthy and effective way to motivate oneself is to use self-compassion, which we'll explore in detail later in the book.

Compassionate Mindful Awareness

Self-Talk

Belief Systems

WHERE DOES THINKING COME FROM?

Whether we're worrying ourselves sick or bullying ourselves, "automatic" thinking is very common. It's our minds way of taking a shortcut to help us navigate through life. In various situations, **our automatic thinking** helps us out hugely. For example, when we meet a new person, we automatically 'know' to greet them with something like "Hi, my name's Louise, nice to meet you". You then might 'know' to ask them their name, and perhaps ask them something like "how are you?". All of these social pleasantries are effortlessly easy, because our thinking minds are guiding us as to what to say. Imagine how difficult life would be without this automation!

I'm going to use this image of the tree to talk about **how we 'grow' our thinking patterns.** If you look underneath the tree, you'll see its root system. In psychology terms, the roots represent our 'belief' systems. Belief systems are very general ways of thinking about the world that get formed way back in our childhood.

When we're born, we're like little blank slates. We have to learn how to walk, and talk, and feed ourselves. We also need to learn how to think.

We **pick up messages** from the people in our environment – our parents, caregivers, siblings, and significant others. In psychological theory, we need to learn what to believe about

1. Ourselves
2. Other people
3. The world

If we're lucky, and we're born into a relatively well adjusted family, and nothing particularly terrible happens to us before the age of about 10, we might pick up some of the following messages from the people around us:

1. "I'm a loveable person" (the self)
2. "Other people are basically trustworthy" (others)
3. "The world is generally a safe place" (the world)

Although belief systems are there, we can't 'hear' them in our day to day lives. But they are constantly influencing how we tend to think about the world. For example, I have a belief system that the world is round. Now, I don't wake up every day and say to myself "OK, the world is round - let's get the day started", but at a very deep, implicit level, I *know* that the world is round, and this belief will subtly influence my experience.

Our general beliefs about ourselves, others, and the world that we develop in childhood give us a **solid foundation**, from which all sorts of thinking can grow. Our belief systems, which we developed as children, dominate the way we think today in our day to day life.

For example, if you have a belief system of yourself as a loveable person, then as an adult, when you meet a potential partner, you might have thoughts like "I think he/she likes me" when you pick up 'I'm interested" signals from the other person. But if you have a belief system "I'm not loveable", then you might not pick up the other person's signals at all, or misread them "There's no way someone like that could like me...he/she must be after my friend". So you can see how our **belief systems** – which get formed way back in our childhoods – can have a huge influence on our lives as adults.

Although belief systems are there, we can't 'hear' them in our day to day lives.

SELF-TALK

If you look at the branches and leaves on the tree, you'll see our self-talk. Self-talk happens in the moment – in our day to day lives. We can actually hear this self-talk if we tune into it – and that's what I teach people to do in therapy – to **tune in and listen** to what we're saying – to what the mind is saying, right now. And as we know, our belief systems greatly influence our self-talk.

Getting to know *how* you speak to yourself is one of the most important goals of psychological therapy. Once you can learn to 'hear' what you're saying to yourself, you can sift through what's useful and helpful, and **identify what's holding you back** or getting you into trouble. We can only change things once we see them – without this perspective, we'll keep getting stuck in unhelpful patterns.

Try a little exercise: what's your mind saying to you right now? What's going on in your self-talk?

FEELINGS

As humans we're always experiencing feelings. Our feelings are different to thoughts, they are the emotional response that arise from our self-talk. For example, if you are thinking "There's no way that handsome man would like me", you might start to feel disappointed, or sad. The feeling that you get is directly caused by your thought.

A simple way to **differentiate a thought from a feeling** is to recognise the chatter and then recognise the response. Often, thoughts arrive in a sentence, like "I shouldn't have eaten that cake." The emotional response is the feeling we get from that thought, and can often be described as one word "Guilt", for example.

Looking at this concept more deeply, the feelings we experience in reaction to our self-talk depend on how much we believe the thought. If you have a thought like "I might take the day off today, and go to the beach",

and you really truly believe it, you might start to feel excited. But if you have exactly the same thought and don't believe it, it won't lead to a strong emotional response.

A lot of our suffering and unpleasant feelings come from believing thoughts. One of the central aims of compassionate mindfulness practice is to **help you to unravel from believing your own thoughts,** to allow thoughts to arrive and then pass, without getting emotionally over-involved with them. In this way, mindfulness can help you to reduce the intensity of unpleasant or difficult emotions.

STOPPING THOUGHTS AND FEELINGS

Most of my clients come to therapy because they want to get rid of their unpleasant thoughts and feelings. This is a bit of a problem, because unfortunately, modern psychology has no way of stopping thoughts from happening. Particularly those thoughts that are very entrenched and automatic – the ones that are quite old. We know that automatic thoughts are a very real

entity, in fact entrenched patterns of thinking even show up on MRI scans. Repetitive thinking patterns result in the brain laying down neural 'tracks' which means that the structure of **the brain itself is changed by how we think.** Pretty amazing, right?

Thoughts that occur a lot are like 6 lane freeways inside our brain – these thoughts have heavy traffic, and are travelled every day. We have no method of 'scrubbing' these neural pathways out of our brains. And even if we could, would we want to? Our thoughts are what makes us human and unique, and our thinking patterns reflect the lives we have lived and the experiences we have had, good and bad combined.

So, we can't 'remove' thinking from our brains. But we *can* work on how we relate to these thoughts, and we can learn to refocus our attention and grow new, more helpful neural pathways which will help us to live differently. This is what compassionate mindfulness practice is all about – changing the structure of our brains to become **calmer, more reflective, and less reactive to the things that happen to us.** We don't need to keep believing old patterns of thinking, even if they keep showing up.

Creating more compassionate responses towards our thinking minds creates new neural tracks in our brains. Over time, and with repetition, these new neural tracks can become alternative to the old pathways.

USING COMPASSION BASED MINDFULNESS TO COPE WITH OUR MINDS

If you look again at the tree diagram, you can see the sun shining on it. The sun is central to compassion based mindfulness – the idea is to pull out of our thinking 'tree' and take a different perspective. When we are anchored in the tree, with all of our self-talk chattering around us, we can't easily see the 'big picture'. Ever heard of the saying 'you can't see the forest for the trees?' This is what it's like when we're constantly in our thinking minds, we are just bombarded with different thoughts and feelings that are all demanding our attention. With so much going on, it's difficult to know what to do. Most of us simply do what the closest or loudest thoughts tell us to do, without taking time to reflect on what we're being told.

Compassionate mindfulness simply means being present, and observing whatever is going on in our thinking minds, without judging whatever is happening. It's 'pulling back' from being in the tree (and stuck in the branches!). From a little further back, we get a different perspective on what's going on.

Once we have a different perspective, we get a fuller understanding of what's going on. From further away, we can see how various thoughts connect with each other, and see where they may have come from. Taking a step back helps us suspend the 'belief' in our thoughts, and this gives us a choice in how we might act.

Warmth

Obviously there is a difference between being in the tree and seeing things from the perspective of the sun. Compassionate mindfulness is about detaching a little from our thoughts, about pulling back.

But remember the sun has warmth to it – it shines on the tree, wanting to nurture it and help it grow. The purpose of compassion based mindful awareness is to retain kindness at all times. Not to look at the tree and judge it, be disappointed in it, or frustrated with its struggles. Compassion based mindfulness is not cold or dismissive... at its heart, it is about wanting the best for your wellbeing.

The Mind Won't Stop Talking & That Doesn't Mean You're Doing It Wrong

A lot of my clients tell me that they've tried mindfulness or meditation before, and that it doesn't work. Melanie, a corporate high flyer with the busiest schedule I've ever seen, told me that she'd tried some meditations before, but found that her mind didn't slow down at all, and she couldn't concentrate. She told me "My mind won't stop, it's no good, I've tried it before".

But that's the best part of compassionate mindfulness – you don't have to stop thinking. In fact, we expect that you'll keep thinking during it. The point of compassionate mindfulness isn't to 'stop' your thinking. Instead, it's to practice the art of *noticing* when you're getting sucked into thinking, and then gently coming back to whatever you're focusing on. Essentially, compassionate mindfulness is about **practising coming back,** rather than expecting that you'll never drift off.

This is why I love compassionate mindfulness so much – when I started my training, my mind was sarcastic, whirled and chatted and argued and daydreamed like there was no tomorrow. I too thought that meditation just wasn't for me: it didn't suit my busy head. But I stuck with it, and found that I could actually detach from all of my crazy thoughts, experiencing a peace I previously hadn't. Yes, my mind is still an expert at pulling me away and making me daydream, but I know that I can manage it and get away from it when I need to. It's wonderfully **empowering!**

So, if you try the exercises in this book and find your mind racing away, you're not doing it wrong. This is what thinking minds do. If you notice that your mind distracts you, simply notice it, accept that it's happened, and re-direct your attention and focus back to the exercise. Some days will be easier than others, and that's ok too.

CHAPTER TWO:

THE BASICS
of
COMPASSION
BASED
MINDFULNESS

IT'S NOT YOUR FAULT

When my clients are starting out with therapy, most of them feel deeply ashamed of themselves because of the contents of their thinking minds. One of the first changes I try to establish is to help people to realise that many of the factors which have created their current experiences were totally beyond their control, and not their fault.

No-one gets to pick their genetic inheritance: it's a lottery. Genes play a significant role in how we are likely to develop psychologically. For example, our genetic predisposition for anxiety or worry, or depression, is coded into us before birth. Evolutionary predispositions towards the 'threat related brain' are extremely common, and because having a worried brain increased our evolutionary chances of survival, it's no surprise that so many of us experience recurring anxiety.

None of us get to choose the family into which we are born. That just happens. The **messages we receive** from the people around us as children, our caregivers' issues and hang ups and ways of dealing with the world - **are beyond our control.** Even the way we interpreted what happened back then wasn't our fault – because we were children, and children's brains are not sophisticated enough to process the myriad of messages given in a nuanced or balanced way.

Harry came to therapy after struggling for many years with persistent depression. He truly believed that he was deeply, fundamentally flawed – that he was 'not good enough'. Harry's father and grandfather had both suffered with severe depression: his inherited genetic vulnerability was apparent. Harry recalled even as a young boy thinking badly towards himself. He related the story of how for many years his father would simply stay in bed and not speak to Harry. These memories were particularly painful for him, he remembered asking his father questions and not even getting a response. As a five year old Harry began to conclude that he was a disappointment to his father, that this was why his dad was depressed – that it was his fault for not being a 'good enough' son.

You can see how easy it would be for the child Harry to view everything as 'his fault'. As children we are very ego centric – we think the world begins and ends with us! It's not until he was much older that Harry was able to get perspective on all of the other factors that might have contributed to his fathers' depression. Still, however, this belief about not being 'good enough' persisted. We worked through this problem in therapy, but this process needed to begin with a recognition that Harry's genetic inheritance and his childhood experiences were *not his fault*. Neither were his conclusions: these were created by his child brain, which was just trying to make sense of his world. Seeing just how much was beyond his control helped Harry to let go of his deeply held conviction that he was 'not good enough', and to begin to see himself through more sympathetic eyes.

By recognising just how much of what goes into making us 'us' is beyond our control, we can start to take a more compassionate and understanding perspective towards ourselves and our difficulties. Keep this in mind as you embark on this path of kindfulness. You're just a human, doing the best you can with whatever you have been given. A lot of what you're going through really isn't your fault.

BEING CURIOUS

When you're starting compassionate mindfulness practice, you'll begin to notice things – a lot of things – that perhaps you haven't before. Some of these will be wonderful, like the mind blowing sweetness of a ripe strawberry, but others may be unpleasant experiences, like feeling very angry or hurt.

Our default is to *judge* these experiences - "that strawberry was amazing! I really liked it – and I want more!" - or "I'm really angry and hurt by what happened today, and I hate feeling like this". This is our **mind's way of helping us to decide what we want to attach to and what we want to get away from**, and in essence it's a very normal, human thing to do.

But constantly labelling our experiences as good or bad means we can lose something important – our objectivity. Scientists who are searching for the cure for cancer don't judge what data they are collecting as good or bad – they simply observe it. And they're generally interested in whatever shows up, because whatever it is, they can learn from it.

Because really, whatever shows up, is there. Being willing to show up, approach, and learn from whatever is arriving is at the heart of being mindful. **There's no right or wrong, there's just experience.**

So, as you're learning and practising compassionate mindfulness skills, do your best to approach whatever shows up with a spirit of curiosity. Be interested in whatever is without becoming too involved in whether or not you like it.

Here's some phrases to use to help cultivate curiosity:

◆ "Well now that's an interesting thing I'm noticing here"
◆ "Wow, look at this!"
◆ "What's this showing me?"
◆ "What's happening here? What can I observe?"
◆ "I'm noticing _____ is happening to me right now"
◆ "I can be open to whatever is happening right now, even if it's not pleasant"

BEING LOVING, GENTLE AND KIND

Another aspect of compassion-focussed mindfulness is to **deliberately cultivate a gentle, caring, and kind attitude** towards your journey of self-discovery. So it's more than simple curiosity towards yourself and the world: it's a position of loving kindness towards yourself and the world.

One way to capture the spirit of this attitude is to **imagine how we feel towards children.** We tend to be particularly kind and loving towards tiny humans, even when they are being difficult. Towards children we are open, non-judgemental, able to view whatever is happening for them through this lens of acceptance and warmth.

This ability of humans to relate to each other in such a kind, compassionate way is immensely important. If we are treated with loving kindness and respect as children, **we feel safe and secure in the world,** able to reach out and explore our environment with a sense of confidence in ourselves. Unfortunately, many people are not so lucky, and grow up feeling judged or criticised in our attempts to live and explore the world.

Compassion based mindfulness asks us to actively foster an attitude of kindness and compassion towards ourselves. This is difficult for many of us, and so within this book there are many practical exercises which will help you to build this skill. It is important to recognise from the outset that this is an intention that you can try to move towards, starting now. Being kind may not be familiar or comfortable right now, but **if you are willing to open up to learning about it,** then that is a great start.

Here are some phrases that you might like to use to start cultivating a sense of kindness:

◆ "What can I say to myself right now, that is kind?"
◆ "Be gentle. Be kind"
◆ "I love and accept myself the way I am, with all of my faults"
◆ "Sending love and kindness to myself right now"

We tend to be particularly kind and loving towards tiny humans, even when they are being difficult.

CHAPTER THREE:

BEING PRESENT

MINDFUL MOMENTS

PAUSING

We hurry through life, busily getting on with everything that we need to do. Only on holidays will we stop to take a breath – and sometimes not even then! This hurry is driven by our attachment to our thinking minds, which are always making us switch attention to the next thing on our 'to do' list.

A fundamental aspect of compassionate mindfulness training is to **slow down.** To pause a little and take things in. To 'check in' and take stock of what is.

COME INTO THE PRESENT

Most of us spend our lives in our tree, without even realising it. The skill of compassionate mindfulness is a very powerful way of getting out of it and finding clarity, peace and direction.

Most of us are constantly engaging with our self-talk, with the thinking mind. Often our minds are talking about something that's in the future, or going over things that have happened in the past. Rarely is the mind **present in the moment that is actually happening right now.** Mindfulness practice is about disengaging from that constant conversation, and putting focus elsewhere.

Mindfulness means being fully present and engaged in the moment. This means **paying attention** to things that are actually happening in the world, *right now*, rather than paying attention to whatever the mind is saying.

A good skill to start with is getting to know where your mind is right now. Let's pause for a moment. Where's your mind at right now? Is it here, with what you are reading now? Or is it wondering what's next? Is it still commenting on the parts you've read before, or what happened yesterday at work?

Ask yourself – where's my head? Is it here, or is in the future/past?

Using Pausing And Being Present In Your Everyday Life

Regular pausing and practising being present gives you the ability to detach from your mind and to get clarity and a sense of peace. You can 'step out' of your tree for a moment, and spend some time in the sun. What a great break!

Opposite are some practical, everyday ideas to get yourself more familiar with 'checking out' of your mind and 'coming into' the present. Pick something on this list, or you can even make your own list:

Pausing tips:

- When you get in the car, before you start the engine, just sit.
- When you wake up in the morning, let yourself lay there for a minute.
- Pause between bites of your lunch.
- At work, between tasks, allow yourself a moment to just sit.
- With your children, rather than rushing, just look at them.
- When getting dressed, let yourself pause between putting on shoes.
- When you're walking somewhere, slow down and see how much time you can take to get to your destination. Deliberately slow down your feet and notice the feeling as your heels and the soles of your feet hit the ground.
- If you're sitting down to check emails, pause a little before you login.

Getting Present:

Once you've paused, practice the following:

1. What's happening right now?
2. How am I going right now?
3. Tell yourself, 'be here, now'....

Here's how it might look. Imagine that you've decided that you'll pause for a moment when you get in the car:

What's happening right now?

"Here I am, sitting in the car. It's Tuesday afternoon. It's a little warm today. I can feel some sweat behind my knees. I can see the trees waving in the breeze. I can hear the radio."

How am I going right now?

"I feel pretty rushed and a little stressed right now".

Be here... now...

In the above, I am noticing only what's happening right now, in the physical world. I'm also checking in with my internal world – my emotional landscape. I'm not judging the moment as good or bad, and I'm not jumping ahead to what's next. I am in the moment, with all of my attention on the here and now.

I often follow up this practice with an acceptance statement - "just this moment". Using this reminds me that whatever is happening in the world and within me, it's OK. It's just a moment, and it won't last.

CHAPTER FOUR:

FOCUS

Compassionate mindfulness is really all about attention. Without mindfulness training, our thinking minds tend to take us over, and we're always paying attention to whatever they are saying. We just blindly go along with whatever our thinking mind is thinking or feeling. But it doesn't have to be this way. We can train ourselves to pay attention elsewhere than the mind. **We can choose where we put our attention.**

To begin compassionate mindfulness practice, I'm going to train you to deliberately place your focus and attention on something other than your busy mind. In this section I'll introduce you to some simple attention practices that will help you to **learn how to attend differently.**

You don't need to do all of them all at once. Give a few of them a go, and over time dip into trying each of them. If you try to do them one after the other you might get overwhelmed!

FOCUS ON THE BREATH

Many people start their compassionate mindfulness practice with breathing meditations. Of course, we are always breathing, but we rarely pay any attention to it. By learning to tune into **the experience of breathing,** we become present in the moment, aware of what is happening.

Below we have an example of an affectionate breathing practice, which is a little different from other mindfulness practices. We start by **focusing on the breath**, and then we introduce an attitude of kindness, affection, and warmth towards ourselves and others. This is a lovely place to start.

There is a script below which you can use to guide you through the meditation. If you like, you could even tape yourself reading this script (using your phone), and then play it back to yourself. If you would prefer to hear my voice guiding you through the meditation, you can download it on itunes using this link: http://itunes.apple.com/album/id1035680975?ls=1&app=itunes

Affectionate Breathing Exercise
Settle yourself into a comfortable position, whether it be lying down, or sitting. Make sure that your body feels fully supported and that you are able to relax. Resting your arms and hands. Allowing your body to soften into a comfortable posture. Gently close your eyes if this feels comfortable for you. Taking a few full, deep breaths to help you to settle into your body. Letting go of any tension as you do this. Feeling your lungs fill up as you breathe in and emptying out as you breathe out.

Now let your breath return to normal. Allowing your breathe to fall into its own natural rhythm, not trying to force it or change it in any way, just **being with whatever feels natural** for your body right now. Simply allow your breathe to breath itself. Allow your attention to be with each inhale and each exhale.

Take a moment now to place your focus on **the place in your body where you most vividly detect the sensations of your breath.** This may be on your nose, or in the nostril, or on your upper lip. Or perhaps in the chest area. Or maybe lower down, towards the bottom of your rib cage. Or even in your tummy. You may simply feel the whole of your body breathing. Wherever the breath is most vividly experienced by you. Allowing your attention to fall onto this place, and following your breath from there.

Imagining your whole body breathing in a gentle, kind, soothing rhythm.

Noticing the changes in sensations as you breathe. As you breathe in, and as you breathe out. As you experience this focus on your breath, you may notice that your mind will wander. To thoughts, images, memories. Your task is not to stop this from happening: as this is what minds like to do. Your task instead is to develop the capacity to notice when your mind is trying to take you away, and to gently turn your attention back to the breath. You might wish to note to yourself, "Ah, this is a thought", and then kindly, and calmly, **return your focus** attention to the breath.

Just this breath in, and this breath out. Allowing your mind to settle into this gentle rhythm of each breath. There is no right or wrong way of breathing, as long as it is comfortable for you.

And now paying attention to your face, to your mouth. Very gently adopt a little tiny smile. Not to create tension, it shouldn't hurt or cause muscle strain, just a very gentle, closed lip, half smile. Notice how it makes you feel when you do this. **Notice what happens to you** when you adopt a facial expression of peace...contentment. Be gentle with this position.

Following the breath now, for a few moments. Being with your breath with full attention. And trying to infuse each breath with a sense of affection... for yourself...for others. Kindness, for yourself and for others. Even if you don't really feel it, try to call up an idea of affection, warmth and kindness. Play with this idea for a little while. Breathing affectionately. Warmly. Kindly. Noticing how that feels.

Breathing in affection and kindness towards yourself. Breathing out affection and kindness towards others, towards the world.

Your mind will definitely wander when you do this. This is normal. It's OK that this happens. And once again, any time that you notice your mind wandering, simply noticing, "Oh, there is a thought", and very gently, and very kindly, bring your attention back to the breath, back to the sensations of your breath as it enters and leaves your body. Back to the intention of kindness and affection.

You might try to put your hand on your heart and feeling the warmth of your hand as it does this. This affectionate gesture as you breathe. Kindness in, kindness out.

Your breath can always **connect you to the present moment**: acting as an loving anchor, to steady you, to tenderly connect you to the here and now. Nothing is wrong, there is only this moment. Only this breath in, and this breath out. **Appreciate your breath for what it is: it brings you life.** Remembering the little half smile. Feeling your hand on your heart, bringing soothing care towards yourself and to the world. Breathe. Kindness towards yourself, and towards others. Let your breath comfort your body with kindness. A gentle flow of kindness and care towards yourself and to the world.

And now allowing this breath to breathe through your whole body. From the tips of your toes to the very top of your head. Kindness and warmth through your whole body. Imagining your whole body breathing in a gentle, kind, soothing rhythm. Keeping in mind this attitude of kindness and affection towards ourselves, and to others as well.

Becoming aware now of the posture of your body as it breathes. And perhaps having a small stretch, and noticing the change in your breath sensations as you do this. And gently allowing yourself to come away from the focus on the breath. Opening your eyes, and coming back to the room. Know that **this affectionate breathing rhythm is always there,** always available for you. All you need to feel anchored to your breath is to focus.

Coming back now, bringing your awareness into your day from now on.

How Was That For You?

This is a question I always ask my clients once we've finished the affectionate breathing mediation. Most of the time, people love it and find it deeply relaxing and peaceful. It's nice to be able to focus away from the mind and onto something as reassuring as the breath.

But affectionate breathing can sometimes make people feel

You may simply feel the whole of your body breathing.

uncomfortable. We're not used to speaking so openly about kindness towards the self. It can feel 'wrong' to be so nice to yourself. This sense of awkwardness or being uncomfortable with affectionate breathing is ok. In our culture we're very wary of being nice to ourselves, seeing it as a weakness. This is strange, as we place a lot of value in being kind and compassionate towards other people – just not ourselves!

Sometimes, affectionate breathing can make people emotional, even tearful. If this happens, that's ok. Being genuinely kind towards ourselves is a deeply vulnerable thing to do, and it's ok if we cry in response to feeling cared for and nurtured. **Allow yourself to be touched by these emotions,** and be kind to yourself. There's nothing wrong with crying.

Some people find that paying attention to their breath is uncomfortable and makes them feel anxious. If that's the case for you, then it can be helpful to anchor yourself in the senses rather than the breath. We'll go through how to do that in the next section.

Affectionate breathing can feel alien and unfamiliar at first, but I encourage you to go with it. We'll be talking a lot more about the science of compassionate mindfulness and how it can help **transform how you're living.** Give it some time. Science is behind you: doing this exercise is very good for your mental health and wellbeing. It's not weak!

How To Use Affectionate Breathing In Your Everyday Life

Practising the affectionate breathing exercises regularly if you can is a great idea. Practical ways to put it into your life might be:

- doing it first thing when you wake up
- doing it when you're about to go to bed
- 'dipping in' to breathing – once you've practised the exercise a few times, it can be useful to try snatching a few affectionate breaths at various times during your day. If you're driving from one place to another, you could try the phrase 'kindness in, kindness out' as you focus on your breath. You can do this for just a few moments, just taking the opportunity to touch base with a kindness anchor.
- placing your hand on your heart or adopting the half smile can also be ways to 'dip into' affectionate breathing. Just before a meeting, take a moment to put your hand on your heart, say 'kindness in/kindness out', and let yourself feel the warmth of your hand as you touch your heart. If you're going to the toilet, do a half smile, touching base with the intent to connect to contentedness and happiness. You don't need huge stretches of time to connect affectionately with yourself. Be creative: when during your day could you 'dip in' to affectionate breathing?

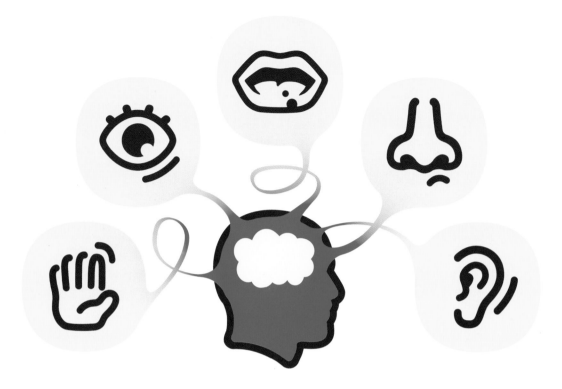

COMING INTO THE SENSES

Coming into the senses is another practice which can help you to get started with compassionate mindfulness.

We have 5 senses: what we can hear, see, smell, touch and taste. **Our senses are always sending us information,** but we don't really tune into it (unless it's something really astonishing, like a strong coffee or a beautiful sunset). We're much more likely to pay attention to our thinking than to what's actually going on in our immediate environment. This is sad, because often in the moment there are some amazing things going on. Mindfulness helps us notice these wonderful moments, increasing our joy.

There is a script below which you can use to guide you through the meditation. If you like, you could even tape yourself reading this script (using your phone), and then play it back to yourself. If you would prefer to hear my voice guiding you through the meditation, you can download it on itunes using this link: http://itunes.apple.com/album/id1035680975?ls=1&app=itunes

Coming Into The Senses Exercise

Sitting comfortably in your chair, take a moment to simply breathe, not trying to change your breathing in any way, just being with your body as it sits and breaths. Once you're feeling centred and ready, go through the following steps:

Step 1. Hearing – pay full attention to everything you can hear right now, in this moment. Let the sounds fall onto your ears, sounds close by and far away. Try not to judge whatever you're hearing as good or bad, pleasant or unpleasant. Simply hear.

Step 2. Seeing – now switch your attention to what you can see. Pick a space in front of you – you might be in front of a coffee table, so focus your sight on the objects on the table. If you are outside, focus on a tree or bush that is close by. Focus all of your attention on the object or objects that you are studying. Notice all of the aspects of shape, colour, light, texture, depth. Again, simply try to see, not judge or give an opinion on what you can see. Give all of your attention to really seeing this object as if it were the first time.

Step 3. Touch: There are a couple of ways you can tune into touch. You may wish to pick up an object, such as a tea cup or a glass, or a pen. Or, you may prefer to focus on how your body is feeling as it sits in the chair you are in. If you are touching an object, bring all of you attention and focus to the feeling of the object in your hands. Is it hot, or cold... smooth or rough... soft, hard... really feeling the object in your hands. If you are connecting with your body, start with your feet on the ground, focusing on how this feels... gradually working your way up your body, your legs, buttocks, back, shoulders, arms, hands, neck and head...noticing the physical sensations of your body in the chair at each level. Either way, allow all of your attention to fall onto what you can touch or feel.

Step 4. Smell: Switching focus now into whatever you can smell in your immediate environment. Taking a moment to inhale deeply to see what you can pick up. It may help to close your eyes to enhance this focus. Notice the temperature of the air that you are breathing in... then notice if there is a scent...or several scents. Noticing without judging whatever smells fall into your senses.

Step 5. Taste: Turning your attention now to inside your mouth, to your tongue and the insides of your cheeks. Noticing the levels of saliva inside your mouth, is there a lot or a little? Trying to detect any tastes, strong or very weak, that are showing up for you. Directing all of your focus into this experience of taste inside your mouth.

Did you notice that your mind got distracted, trying to pull you away? That's OK, remember getting off focus is part of being human.

How Was That For You?

Many of my clients say that this simple exercise is amazing...that they hadn't noticed just how much is going on in the moment. By attending to the senses, we get to experience what really IS happening, rather than running off with our minds into the future. It's lovely and peaceful in most moments when we can attend to the senses...

A lot of my clients also say that one sense will be more compelling or 'speak' to them more than others. For me, coming into what I can smell is very powerful, I'm able to really focus on whatever scents are arising and this captures my attention, making it easier for me to focus away from my thinking mind. Others are different: some clients are visual, some love hearing as their major focus.

Using Coming Into The Senses In Everyday Life

If you find that one sense stands out for you more than others, it can be helpful to practice 'coming into' that sense several times a day, to get into the habit of 'grounding' yourself in that sensory moment. Build it into your day, into your life. If it's sound, ask yourself "What can I hear right now?"....

All around my house (and at my workplace) I have various exotic smells to help me come into the moment. I have oriental lilies at home, because I love the amazing smell. When my gardenias bloom, I pick them and put them next to my bed. At work, we have scented candles burning almost all of the time.

MINDFUL BODY AWARENESS

We live in our bodies, but unless we're in a lot of pain, or feeling a lot of pleasure, it's easy to tune out. Developing the art of paying attention to your body is amazing and rewarding. Not only will you learn to re-connect with your body, you'll learn to appreciate it and care for it in a way that perhaps you haven't before.

Enjoy these exercises which can help you to focus on the wonder of your own body.

1. Put a favourite artwork print up in your workplace (for visual people)

2. Each time you go outside, choose an everyday object to study like you've never seen it before (for visual people)

3. Get a favourite piece of music on your iPod or put it in your car (for hearing people)

4. Identify sounds you particularly like and try to get close to them (e.g., if you like the sound of birds, go to the park at lunch time) (for hearing people)

5. Buy a fluffy cushion and put it next to you on the couch (for touch people)

6. Get hold of a special touch object (e.g., a smooth cold stone, or a textured necklace) and carry it in your handbag. Touch it periodically throughout the day (for touch people)

7. Get to know smells that you love, and put them into your house and workplace (e.g., flowers, candles, leather) (for smell people)

8. When you're outside, breathe in the air and notice the number of different smells that are around (for smell people)

9. For the first bite of every meal or snack, pay full attention to the taste and sensations in your mouth (for taste people)

10. Each time you drink, notice the texture, feel and taste (for taste people)

By attending to the senses, we get to experience what really IS happening.

YOUR AMAZING LEFT ARM

Bring all of your attention and awareness to your left arm. Start at the shoulder, and then slowly drag your focus down your arm towards your elbow. Bring an intention of kindness, gentleness, and lovingness towards this focus. Notice all of the sensations in this area of your body. Notice warmth, or coolness. Tension or relaxation. Now to your elbow, holding your attention there for a moment. Appreciating how your arm feels at this junction. And now further down still, through your forearm, towards your hand. Notice again warmth, or coolness. Tension or relaxation. **Sending kindness, gentle loving attention.** And now to your left hand. Starting at the wrist, cast your attention across the back of your hand. Notice how the back of your hand is feeling right now. Warmth, or coolness. Tension or relaxation. And now up your pinky finger, starting at the base where it joins with your hand. Very slowly up, and up. Noticing all the way, warmth, or coolness. Tension or relaxation. Reaching the joint now... and through and up still towards the nail. And pull back slightly to become aware of all of your pinky finger, in all of its exquisite detail. Feeling affectionate towards your pinky.

Now turning to the next finger, starting at the base where it meets your hand. Noticing fully the sensation in your finger as you slowly start to travel up towards the joint. Again noticing warmth, or coolness. Tension or relaxation. And pausing at the joint, pouring all of your focus and attention to the middle joint in this finger. And then travelling further up, towards the next joint, and all the way up to your fingertip, noticing all of the sensations at the tip of this finger right now. Pull back slightly to take in the sensations of the whole finger, bringing a spirit of loving kindness to the awareness.

And now gently turning your attention to the middle finger. Starting at the base, slowly taking your focus up towards the joint. Notice warmth, or coolness. Tension or relaxation. At the joint now, pause and softly let yourself observe all of the sensations in this tiny area of your body. Now travelling further up the finger, towards the next joint, and up to the fingertips and nail. **Feeling how it feels in this moment,** the whole finger. Bringing a sense of kindness towards this attention.

And now back to the index finger, starting where it meets your hand and slowly travelling upwards towards the joint. Observing warmth, or coolness. Tension or relaxation. Gentle awareness now at the joint, pausing a little to notice any sensations occurring. And then up, to the next joint, and then the fingertips. Just noticing... and then pulling back to kindly, lovingly observe the index finger in its entirety.

Then to your thumb. Starting at the base once again, noticing warmth, or coolness. Tension or relaxation. Travelling upwards towards the joint, pause at the joint. Gently notice the sensations. Then dragging the focus up towards the tip of your thumb. Sitting for a moment and resting with **full conscious awareness** in the whole of your left thumb. Feeling kindness towards your hard working thumb.

Notice all of the sensations in this area of your body.

Pull back even further to observe the sensations in the whole of your hand. All of the fingers, the thumb, the back and front of your hand. Notice warmth, or coolness. Tension or relaxation. Noticing all of this with kindness. And pull back further to notice the who of your left arm and hand. All the way from your left shoulder, down your left arm, to the elbow, through the forearms, to the hand. Noticing with all of your awareness the many sensations occurring in your left arm right now. And bringing an intention of soft, loving awareness into this practice.

MINDFUL MOVEMENT

A really nice way of getting present is to experiment with moving your body in small ways and paying full attention to that. This can be done anywhere, anytime, and it's a great way of grounding yourself when things are tough. I particularly like this way of becoming mindful, as it connects you with your amazing body. We are so used to moving our body that we have lost the sense of **how incredible and nuanced moving really is.** I find this type of mindful moment endlessly fascinating.

Below is an exercise to start you off. I've used the left arm as an example, but don't feel limited by my choice. If you'd prefer to use a different body part, that's fine. You don't have to move a lot in order to experience it: you could even practice with shutting and opening your eyes. Whichever bit of the body you're choosing, just try to follow the general principles of **moving the body part slowly and paying full attention to it.**

Moving Your Amazing Left Arm

Sit down and rest your arms comfortably in your lap. Consciously bring your attention towards your left arm. Now, staying focussed on your left arm, slowly lift it up. Very slowly, very deliberately. As you do this, do your best to really notice each and every muscle that is involved in helping you to lift your arm. Bring an attitude of gratitude towards your body for allowing you to do this.

Notice the shoulder muscles, the muscles in your biceps and triceps. The change in your forearms and hands as you lift. The sense of strain, or pressure, or tension that arises in your arm as it moves. Be gentle towards this strain. Notice the sensations of the air around your arm as you move it.

Lift the left arm up until it is at shoulder height. Hold it there for a little moment, noticing the sensations involved in holding your arm extended and still.

Then very slowly, play with bending and then straightening your elbow. Straighten the arm, until you are sitting with your left arm extended straight out in front of you. Now bend it, bringing your hand back in close towards your face. Do each of these movements exquisitely slowly, and pay all attention and focus to the sensations in your arm that arrive and shift as you do this movement. Notice with a very gentle quality of awareness just **how much your body responds to your desire to move.** Thanking your body for moving in this way.

Now with your arm straight out in front of you again, gently twist your palm up so it faces the ceiling. Now twist again until your palm is facing the floor. Noticing the change in sensations that occur as you do this movement. Notice the tension and strain in your arm that this motion causes. Once again, **sending a message of kindness** towards your body, thanking it for helping you.

Straightening out your arm once more, and with your palm towards the ceiling, practice clenching your hand into a fist, and then straightening your fingers, stretching them straight, and then again into a clench. Repeat this several times, staying with attention towards the difference in sensation between the closed fist and the open hand. Holding an attitude of gentle curiosity towards these sensations.

And then allowing yourself to move your arm back down towards your lap. Moving slowly still, keeping your focus on the sensations that occur in your left arm as it moves downwards. Finally to resting in your lap, let go of any tension and allow your lap to cradle your arm. Notice the sense of relaxation in your left arm.

Sending warmth and gentle thanks towards your left arm for moving according to your wishes. For a moment focus on just how much goes into moving your arm. Allow yourself to **feel the glorious complexity of your body, and being grateful for it.**

I find this type of mindful moment endlessly fascinating.

How Was That For You?

I hope that focusing on your body in a more compassion-focussed mindful manner has been an eye opener for you. Paying attention in this way highlights that there are many **alternative places to put your attention other than your 'tree'.**

Paying mindful attention to the body not only helps us to step out of our minds, it also encourages physical relaxation. By showering our body with caring attention, we effortlessly let go of any physical tension, creating **a lovely sense of calm and looseness.** Physical relaxation tends to settle the mind, slowing down anxiety related 'racing' thoughts. Getting into the habit of mindfully paying attention to your body has a multitude of benefits.

Some clients are experiencing painful problems with their bodies: perhaps chronic pain, or illness, or injuries, which can affect their focus. If you are in pain, mindful awareness of the body can conjure up difficult thoughts related to the injury or pain.

But simply building this intention to pay attention to the body in a non-judgemental way, pain and all, can help you to **relax around the pain,** thereby reducing or minimising the amount of pain felt. If you are experiencing pain, I would encourage you to still do the body awareness practice, with the intention not to make the pain go away, but to sit with it more comfortably. Of course, if the experience is too overwhelming or painful, try another method of developing your focus, such as the senses. Compassionate mindfulness should not make you feel worse, it should make you feel better!

Please don't limit yourself to paying attention to your left arm. Extend the practice and focus to your whole body. I haven't put the entire body into this book in the interests of brevity, but a whole body mindfulness meditation is available on my Building Self-Compassion album, available on itunes at http://itunes.apple.com/album/id1035680975?ls=1&app=itunes

Extend the practice and focus to your whole body.

Using Your Body As A Focus In Everyday Life

If you have resonated with paying attention to the body, you can use it to help you 'dip in' to compassionate mindfulness during your day.

Like the senses, there may be a part of your body that 'speaks' to you more than another. If this is the case for you, you can use this place as a way to 'hook in' to becoming mindful.

For me, my left arm stands out. This is perhaps because I am left handed, and as I write a lot, it becomes fatigued easily. So in my life I spend a lot of time paying attention to how this part of my body is going. In this way, I have learned to relax my body and therefore switch off the stress response.

Here are some ways to step into the body during your daily life:

♦ Choose a regular activity that you do each day. It might be: sending an email or text message, doing the washing up, or walking to the bus stop.

♦ As my job is very 'mental' rather than physical, I spend each day detached from my body. At the end of a day of clients, I choose to sit for a moment to re-connect with my body.

♦ Use this activity as a cue to tune into the area of your body that 'speaks to you.

♦ When you do the activity, ask yourself "how is my _____ feeling now?"

♦ Spend a few moments scanning this part of your body. I start at my shoulder and scan down towards the elbow, and then the forearm, down to the hand, and each finger.

♦ Notice sensations...hot or cold...tense or relaxed. Just seeing what is there, not requiring it to change. "Notice...."

♦ Sending an intention of gratitude towards your body for holding you, looking after you, and being there for you. "Thankyou..."

CHAPTER FIVE:

COMPASSIONATE MINDFULNESS *in* EVERYDAY LIFE

We have looked at how compassionate mindfulness is really **a process of directing our attention** to what is really happening in this moment. Our boring everyday lives are stuffed full of opportunities to become more compassionately mindful.

Since I started to practice compassionate mindfulness, I have experienced more joy. This is not because my life has changed remarkably: it's still the same. I am still raising two kids. I still go to work. I cook, do the school drop offs, and run my business. I do the groceries. I clean the house. I watch TV. I see friends and family when I can. I walk, run, and play softball. Much of my life is like "Groundhog Day" - same old, same old. But compassionate mindfulness has given me a exceptional gift – to experience **the wonder, joy and appreciation of the everyday.** I used to think that I would feel more joy when my life changed (when the kids are older, when I had more money, when I was fitter etc.). I have now discovered that nothing in my life needs to change, in order for everything to change.

Let me explain more clearly: dipping into kindful awareness on a daily basis has helped me connect with the absolute wonder of the present moment. Everyday things that used to fly under the radar are now **opportunities** to experience something fantastic. I encourage you to try one or all of the following, to really drop into a sensory awareness of the moment. Each moment is priceless, rich and dripping with meaning.

This chapter is all about finding new ways to **connect with the everyday**. I hope you find it useful. Like the last chapter, don't feel compelled to do everything here all at once. Dip in and try out the activities that make the most sense to you.

MINDFUL BOREDOM: FINDING JOY IN THE MUNDANE

I used to despise doing the washing up, thinking that it was a terrifically boring daily task which just annoyed me. Learning compassionate mindfulness changed that. By tuning into what was actually happening – and by **choosing not to focus on my thinking mind's negative judgements** of it – I really started to notice a whole range of things. The smell of the lemony detergent. The warmth of the water through my gloves. The feeling of the plates, glasses, and cups on my fingers. The sound of gentle clanking. All of this glorious sensory experience! Now, I take the opportunity to wash up whenever I can...I look forward to it as a really nice 'break' from my own mind.

Is there a boring everyday task which you can choose to approach more mindfully? Here are some suggestions:

◆ Mindful driving
◆ Mindful shower
◆ Mindful nappy change (yes it is possible!)
◆ Mindful emailing or texting
◆ Mindful vacuuming
◆ Mindful tooth brushing
◆ Mindful hair brushing
◆ Staring at carpet

MINDFUL WALK

Think of the last time you went for a walk. You might have been on your way somewhere, or perhaps you simply went walking. How much did you notice about the walk?

Most of the time when we walk, we're not really there. Our minds are at it as usual: talking to us about where we're going, worrying about if we'll get there on time, running through what needs to get done. Or maybe dwelling on something a friend said to you the other day, or comparing yourself to the jogger running past you....

This chatter distracts us from the moment. **Walking can be such an amazing experience, when it's done mindfully.** So next time you go for a walk, really *go*. This means doing your best to tune out from your thinking mind and dropping into the sense. What can you see, hear, smell, feel, touch?

Be there in the act of walking. **Feel your legs** leave the ground, swing forward and reconnect with the earth. Notice your breath. Feel the rhythm of walking. Connect with the sense of your feet on the ground, lifting and falling back.

Use your eyes to **study what you can see**, allowing everything to fall into your field of vision. See what is far away: look up at the sky, the clouds. Get up close to things. Lean in and really *look* at a flower or a plant.

Take in the intricate detail of this plant, this flower. Observe the colours, shapes, and textures.

Touch things. Touch plants, petals, bark. Observe the temperature: cool, warm, or hot. Feel the textures hitting your fingers. Smell deeply: **inhale and notice whatever you can sense.** Feel the environment around you – the sense of sun on your shoulders, or rain, or shade, cool, cold or warm.

Be aware of your body as it walks, does it feel looser, warmer? Is your heart beating more strongly? Notice exertion if you go up a hill. Notice pull on your body if you walk down a hill.

If your mind distracts you during the walk (which it will – minds like to pull us away from moments), that's OK. Simply noticing the distraction and very gently, kindly coming back to your senses, what you can notice.

MINDFUL WATER

I am lucky enough to live right near the beach. When the weather is warm, one of my favourite things to do is to go for a swim, mindfully. If you are lucky enough to be able to swim, and you have access to water, then I invite you to **try out a mindful swim.**

Swimming is a joyful activity, and it's an easy way to get mindful. Because the experience is so pleasant, and so sensory, it's a very accessible way to start tapping into mindful living. Once again, the emphasis is on falling into the senses – what you can feel, touch, see, hear, taste, and smell – and tuning out of the thinking mind.

I walk down the beach towards the water, feeling the hot sand underneath my toes. Towards the edge of the water the sand is noticeably cooler, and much more firm. The sun is out, it's a beautiful 30 degree day, and the waves are smooth. The water is aqua and blue, and the sun sparkles like diamonds on the waves as they build up and crash. I can hear the laughter of children and the shouts of the lifesavers as they train further up the beach. The drone of the seaplane as it flies overhead.

The water hits my toes, and it's a shock of coldness. I can smell salt, seaweed. I walk further into the water, the waves hitting my body. I can feel the current dragging me in. The coldness travels up my body and my skin is tingling, feeling fresh and alive and vital. I can see water, waves, other swimmers. The white foam of the waves and sand in the water, clouding it. I take a breath in and duck under the wave, feeling another cold shock to my head and face, and the resultant tingly afterglow.

I float on my back, toes up towards the waves, watching myself bob in the water. **Feeling weightless, fluid.** Hearing the water in my ears. Watching my toes and the waves behind them. Feeling cool, refreshed.

If you can't swim, or you don't have access to a beach, lake, river, or pool, try getting mindful in water by having a shower or a bath.

MINDFUL EATING

Eating is something we do several times a day. Again, it's one of those activities that is so familiar that we easily 'tune out'. We eat until the plate is clean, then we move on. Food is also a source of guilt for a lot of us, so in this way our thinking minds can get in the way and 'ruin' our enjoyment and pleasure.

I think tuning out is a crime against food! When we get mindful, the act of eating is intense, beautiful, and rewarding. Many of my clients say that they can't believe **how enjoyable eating can be.** It also tends to be that when we pay true attention, we often don't need to eat as much as we habitually do.

To get started with mindful eating practice, choose a delicious food that you love to eat. If you're not sure, then try this out with a piece of fruit which is in season and wonderfully ripe. I'm choosing a gorgeous little cherry tomato, my favourite in-season fruit.

Once you have your food ready, set aside a little time for you to do this exercise – you'll need 15 or so minutes of uninterrupted time. Put the food on a plate and sit down in front of it.

Check in with your **hunger levels.** How interested in food is your body right now? Are you a little hungry...very hungry? Not hungry at all? Perhaps full?

If you are very hungry, it might be difficult for you to do this exercise. Perhaps have a snack and then try the mindfulness exercise about 15 minutes later. If you're overly full, wait a little while until you're slightly hungry. Slightly hungry is the best time to do a mindfulness exercise as your body will send you extra special enjoyment signals!

I'm slightly hungry, which is just right...

Now, really look at the food in front of you. Study it with your eyes as if you've never seen this food before. Notice its appearance.

My cherry tomato is red, very red. I have cut it in half, and on the inside I see the little white stripe down the middle, with seeds sitting in the middle, looking juicy. The tomato is oval in shape, and small. It's sitting there on the plate, looking tempting.

Now try to touch the food with your fingers. Pick it up, if it's small enough, and feel the texture and temperature of it. Or simply run your fingers along the food if it's not easy to pick up.

I pick up one half of the cherry tomato and run my finger underneath it. Its underside is curved. The flesh feels plump and full. The skin feels cool, smooth. I touch the topside of the tomato and notice this side is moist, cool, slightly slimy, and delicately bumpy where the seeds are.

Now smell this food. Smell is a powerful communicator, one which we overlook. Put your nose close and inhale the smell, picking up in detail the aromas that are emanating from the food. It may help to close your eyes while you do this so you can focus your full attention on the smell.

I pick up the tomato and hold it under my nostril, inhaling. The tomato smells fresh, cool, and – tomato-like! It sounds weird but I can smell the skin. Over the seeds there is a delicate, slightly more citrus smell that is different to the skin. I notice while I smell that **my mouth is starting to salivate,** and I am experiencing a desire to eat it!

Now it's time to taste. Take a mouthful of the food – a comfortable bite size. Slowly start to chew. Notice the flavours on your tongue as you chew. **Feel the food inside your mouth,** noticing any changes in sensation as the food breaks down. Notice the food between your teeth as they grind the food. Just notice what is happening. When you get the urge to swallow, do so, noticing how it feels to do so. See if more changes in flavour happen after you swallow. Notice any aftertaste that lingers in your mouth.

I put the tomato in my mouth and begin to chew. I crunch through the tough skin and feel the softer inside of the tomato, and the runny seeds. The flavour is astringent, tangy. My mouth fills with slightly sweet water. As I chew the soft bits disappear and my teeth are left with the tougher skin, which breaks up and sits between my teeth. I keep crunching and swallow it down. After it goes I can feel the aftertaste in the middle of my tongue, and some remnants of skin still in my teeth.

After I eat, I spend a moment or so contemplating with **gratitude.** This tomato was grown at a farm, and many hands have gone into its creation. I am for a moment taken aback by **a sense of enormous privilege.** I am so lucky to be able to eat such delicious food so effortlessly.

SEX

We've talked about how not paying attention to the everyday things, such as eating or moving our bodies reduces enjoyment. Guess what? The same applies to sex. You can have a much **more enjoyable, joyful, and adventurous time with sex and intimacy** when you use compassionate mindfulness.

We are physical beings, with sexual desires and interests. Over time, our minds learn about sex, too: what we like, don't like, etc. Inside our heads we have a **'sex folder'** that we internally refer to when we think about sex. If it's full of positive, rewarding memories and fantasies, we're likely to enjoy a stress-free and enjoyable, relaxed sexual life. But if the folder has some not-so-great memories, or if the folder is connected to 'feeling stressed', or 'feeling bored', we can run into trouble in the bedroom.

Here are some steps that you can take to make your sex life more compassionate, mindful and aware. The steps below are written for two people, but you can easily do the steps alone.

1. Foster an attitude of willingness, openness and curiosity

We all have pre-conceived ideas about sex and intimacy, both with regards to ourselves, and to our partners. The first step is to work on getting out of your 'tree' and into the sun – looking down at the various thoughts, feelings, and memories that pop up when you start to **think about having sex or getting physical.** Let yourself see what comes up, without getting too attached to them. You might notice thoughts such as "I'm too tired!", or "I'm not going to enjoy it...", or "I'm too fat to get naked". Let yourself see the thoughts that might be getting in the way of your willingness to put yourself

in a sexual situation. You need to get a good understanding of **what's in your sexual 'folder'.** Is it generally positive and open towards sex, or is it more unwilling, not excited, not interested?

There's no right or wrong here – there's simply seeing, and noticing. If you are seeing a whole bunch of negative, anxious, fearful thoughts about sex, it might not be a bad idea to seek some help from a qualified therapist.

If you genuinely want to explore a more compassionately mindful way to approach sex, then it can help to develop **an attitude of willingness and curiosity, and openness,** to the whole area. This might be quite different to what you're used to.

Being willing to be sexual is different to feeling the desire to be sexual. Desire is a type of arousal – it's a pull, an interest – in being sexual, which is physically based. **Willingness to be sexual,** on the other hand, is cognitively based – it's more of an intellectual decision to be sexual, even if desire isn't there. For many of us, low desire can be a problem. Low desire comes from familiarity, from being tired, from being affected by the myriad of life stressors that take away our mojo. If you have low desire, but you have willingness to be sexual, that's a great place to start. Desire can build from mindfulness practice: willingness is the choice that you make right here, right now.

So, if you're willing to be more sexual, then it's OK to start - even if you're not bubbling over with desire.

So we've established that you're willing to **explore and connect with your sexuality.** Now make sure that you're willing to step into this practice with your partner (if you have one). This might mean letting go of some of the negative thoughts about them, letting go of the prediction that the sex won't be good, letting go of thoughts about your body. Step into willingness. Lean into this experience, with this person. Let yourself be open to the experience you are going to have right now, without connecting to expectations or memories. Let it just be as it will.

Be curious – allow yourself to be interested and not judgemental towards whatever will happen. With an attitude of curiosity, it's easier to stay open.

2. Set the mood

Sex is a sensory experience. Using what you have learned about which of the senses appeal to you, take some time to **create an atmosphere** that will encourage your desire. If you are a visual person, this might mean having a tidy room, or going somewhere visually pleasing. If you like scent, change the sheets, or put some scented candles on. If you like sounds, put on music.

Make sure that you have **ample time to explore mindful sex:** don't do this exercise 15 minutes before you're due at work! Ideally, set aside a whole evening (or morning, if that's a better time for you).

3. Anchor in the body

Allow yourself a few moments to focus on anchoring your awareness in your body. Rather than letting your mind direct this process, you'll be paying attention to physical sensations and letting yourself be in this moment.

Invite your partner to join you, and ask him/her to **anchor in the breath** as a way for both of you to get started. You might want to lay comfortably in each other's arms, or side by side. Whatever feels right.

Take a few deep breaths in and out to get started. You might want to close your eyes as you do this, to really pay attention to how your breath is feeling as it enters and leaves your body.

Then allowing your breathing to return to its natural rhythm, not trying to change it or force it. Just let your attention be with that breath.

4. Looking

With your partner, sit or lie so you are facing each other at a distance that feels natural for you. Take a moment now to **look at each other**...really look. See into your partners eyes. Seek connection in that gaze. Allow your breathing to settle as you sink into this moment of really looking at your partner. Notice how it feels to look... notice how it feels to be seen.

Connect with your emotions of attachment, love and care towards this person. Let go of any petty thoughts, disagreements, arguments or faults. **Focus attention on the love,** the connection between you. Here is your partner, your love. Who loves you.

5. Breathe into your sexy bits

Still looking at your partner, next time you take a breath in, bring your attention and focus to your genitals. Feeling the **blood flow** into your vagina or penis with each in breath. Letting yourself anchor your attention in your genitals. Noticing any differences that happen in your body as you move attention to your vagina

or penis. Being open to sensations of heat, or tingling. Noticing arousal and desire, if it arrives. If you need to, close your eyes and focus all of your attention here.

A really enjoyable way to experience breathing into your genitals is through massage. Take turns to give each other a ten minute massage. Lie on your front and enjoy the experience of your partner gently (or firmly, whatever way you like it) rubbing oil into your back. With your eyes closed, really **pay attention to the sensations of warm hands** on your back. And as you are breathing, on the 'in' breath, take it all the way down to your genital area. Focus your attention on the sensations of breath going into this area. Let yourself notice the changes in your sensations as you let yourself breathe into a state of desire. Letting go of any thoughts that arrive, and gently coming back to the practice of breathing down into your genitals.

6. Play with touch

Slowly, and with awareness, start to experiment with touching your partner and with being touched. Or touching yourself. Start in **a place where you feel comfortable and safe being touched** – not the genitals.

Experiment with kissing, with different intensity, with and without tongues. If you are being touched, notice the feeling on your skin.

Be with the sensations. **Really feeling, and experiencing** this touch as if it was the first time, as if the experience was totally new. If something is not pleasant, gently say "no".... if something is pleasant, gently say "yes"...and respond in kind with your partner.

Don't let yourself touch or be touched in the genital area until you are feeling fully aroused. You'll know you're aroused if you have an erection (if you're male), or if your genitals are swollen and slightly pink, perhaps with vaginal lubrication (if you're female). Allow your deep breathing and the experience of touch in other areas of your body to create sexual arousal in your genitals...and then start touching. It's like allowing yourself to be hungry before you eat. If you allow sexual arousal to happen before touch occurs, you'll have a much more enjoyable and mind blowing experience!

7. Pay attention to the senses

Keep coming back to the experience of sensations, of warmth or coolness, of touch, and let yourself be in this physical place. Let yourself look at your partner, at your body, at both of you together. Connect with the love, care and connection between you.

When you notice that your mind is starting to drag your attention away – by judging, by going into the future, by connecting with the past – gently notice this, and without too much effort, **gently come back to the moment.** To the breath in, and the focus on drawing your breath down towards your genitals. Grounding yourself in growing desire.

Let things take their course, going at a pace that feels right for you. There are no rules as to what happens next. Go with what **feels instinctively right.** Be curious, and open to whatever is happening. Letting yourself go with the flow of touch and response. Enjoy!

Being willing to be sexual is different to feeling the desire to be sexual.

CHAPTER SIX

TAKING IT DEEPER:

Compassionate Mindfulness of Your Thoughts

So far we have looked at how to become compassionately mindful by diverting our attention away from our minds, and onto other things: the present moment, or the body, or the senses, or the breath. This type of focussed attention gives us a way to get out of our minds by **anchoring ourselves in something real** that is happening in the moment. We are now going to look at how mindfulness can be used to relate to our thinking in a different way.

Becoming more mindful of our thoughts and feelings is a wonderful skill. Rather than living in our tree, through mindful awareness we develop the ability to pull out and observe this internal landscape, without getting overly attached to whatever is happening there. When we **learn to detach** in this way we're better able to make decisions based on what's best for us, on what's likely to make us happy, rather than making decisions based on whatever our mind happens to be hung up on.

Compassionate mindfulness is a powerful way of relating to your thinking mind. Throughout our lives we are strongly attached to whatever we are thinking or feeling. But this strong attachment can make things difficult – it can increase our suffering. This idea is at the heart of psychological therapy: **it's not our thoughts that cause us pain**, it's the strength of our attachment to these thoughts that cause pain.

Mary came to see me after suffering debilitating panic attacks for the last 6 months. Every time she experienced **panic symptoms**, she would have terrible thoughts such as "I'm going crazy". She truly believed that she was losing her sanity. Her belief in this thought increased her anxiety and panic, creating a vicious cycle of spiralling panic.

In therapy, we discussed the genetic origin and physiology of panic attacks, and how they are a very common human experience. I explained to her that although the panic symptoms were very intense and frightening, she certainly was not going crazy. Once Mary was able to understand what she was experiencing, she felt relieved. She realised that because of her genetic predisposition to anxiety, and her family history, it really wasn't surprising that she was suffering from panic. It really wasn't her fault.

Over the next few days, she continued to experience panic attacks, however she found that when the thought "I'm going crazy" popped up, she didn't quite believe it as much as she had previously. Mary was already taking a more **compassionate, understanding perspective towards her experiences.** Subsequently, her panic around going crazy stopped, and the spiralling stopped.

Compassionate mindfulness gives us a way to detach from unhelpful thoughts. Firstly, we have to notice that something is happening. We can **'pause'** to see what's going on. Imagine that you are the sun, looking down towards your tree. What thoughts can you see?

Here are some useful questions you can use to start the process:

◆ What am I thinking?
◆ What's going on for me right now?
◆ What's my head saying?

Trying of course not to judge whatever your thoughts are saying, but simply to observe, to notice, in a curious way. To do this objectively, as if there were no right or wrong way to think – there are simply thoughts.

To help you maintain objectivity you might try the following phrases:

◆ Ah, there's a thought:
◆ My head is saying :
◆ My thoughts are telling me that....
◆ It's just a thought....

In compassionate mindfulness the overarching theme is to **let go of our bias and judgements** about whatever we are going through at the time, and to simply let it be. We need to accept that the mind can be a pretty outrageous place, and all sorts of weird and wonderful things can be said in there. But regardless of whatever we are thinking, it's all ok, because they are just thoughts, and we are just humans.

Thoughts are not necessarily true, or helpful, or useful. But they are there, and that is that. To struggle with whether or not they should be there is pretty pointless, because the fact is the thought is there, like it or not. So we can gain a lot from just accepting that it's there.

Becoming more mindful of our thoughts and feelings is a wonderful skill.

ACCEPTING THOUGHTS & NOTICING JUDGEMENT

If we struggle with thoughts, we actually **add to our pain.** Sophie was a yoga teacher who had come to see me for help with her perfectionism and the anxiety that this brought about. She was familiar with the principles of mindfulness from her yoga practice. However, her mind was wracked with judgemental thoughts. When we ran through mindful awareness of her thoughts, Sophie would notice things such as "I've got to get better at mindfulness or I'll be a terrible yoga teacher". Understandably, her attachment to this thought made her feel quite terrible. But then her mind would throw more judgement at her as a result of noticing this thought! "I can't believe I'm having such stupid thoughts! I'm such an idiot!"

So here, Sophie was able to notice her thoughts, but rather than accepting them, her mind added to her pain by **judging her thoughts.** I call this 'level 2' judgement. Level 1 judgement is the original thought ("I've got to get better at mindfulness or I'll be a terrible yoga teacher"), level 2 judgement is the critical response that the mind has about the thought. Level 1 thoughts can make us feel pretty bad, but add level 2 judgement and the original bad feeling is even worse.

Level 2 judgement is very common, and very unhelpful. Judgement simply tries to say that whatever is there shouldn't be there. This is the very opposite of **acceptance,** which allows whatever is there to be there.

Imagine being in a traffic jam. There you are, stuck in a long line of cars that aren't moving anywhere. You have no choice in being in the traffic jam: there it is, and there you are, in it. Your only choice in this scenario is how you deal with it.

1. You can rage: "How is this even possible?! This should NOT be happening! This is absolutely ridiculous, these idiots should get off the road...."

2. You can accept: "Here is a traffic jam, and I'm in it". It's not my favourite thing in the world, but here it is anyway.

The phrase 'radical acceptance' was coined by Tara Brach. It means clearly recognising whatever is going on in the **present moment** and relating to that experience with compassion. We'll be talking a lot more about compassion shortly, but for now, the idea is to absolutely accept whatever thoughts you notice, whether you **like them or not.**

Here are some useful phrases to use to help you gain acceptance of your thoughts:

◆ It's ok for me to be thinking that....

◆ This thought is here right now

◆ I'm alright with the thought that....

◆ I accept that I am having this thought....

◆ All thoughts are ok

LOOSENING FROM THOUGHTS

The leaves on a stream meditation presented below is a very lovely way to introduce yourself to noticing, accepting and **letting go** of thoughts as they occur. Give yourself some time to sit somewhere quiet and experience this meditation.

Feel free to record yourself reading this script (using your phone), and then play it back to yourself. If you would prefer to hear my voice guiding you through this meditation, you can download it on itunes using this link: http://itunes.apple.com/album/id1035680975?ls=1&app=itunes

Leaves On A Stream

Settle yourself into a comfortable position, however that feels right for you. Making sure that your body feels comfortably supported and that you are able to soften and relax. And gently closing your eyes. Allow your body to **sink into this moment.**

Focusing now on your breath, on the sensation of your breath as it enters and leaves your body. Not trying to change your breath in any way, just being with it and noticing with a gentle quality of kindness how your lungs feel as they fill up and let go. Let your breath fall into its own natural rhythm.

And now turning your attention and focus towards your internal experience. Towards your thoughts. Our minds are almost always busy with thoughts, they are rarely quiet. Today we'll use **a visualisation** technique to help you deal with this thinking mind of yours.

Imagine that you are sitting peacefully next to a stream. Take a moment to conjure up an image of a stream in **your mind's eye.** And of you sitting on its banks. It might be a large stream, or it may be small. It could be somewhere you've been before, or something you're just making up as you go. It's OK, it's your stream, let the image pop up. Imagine that you are feeling very rested and comfortable here beside the stream, just sitting and watching the water flow by.

As you are watching the water, you notice that there are leaves floating upon its surface. There are leaves of all different shapes and sizes. Leaves of all different colours.

As you are focusing on these images, you might notice that your **thoughts are trying to distract you.** This is totally normal – this is what thoughts love to do. But rather than doing what comes naturally and getting lost in thought, we are going to try something different.

Next time you become aware of a thought popping into your head, imagine that you could somehow **take the thought outside of your mind,** and place it gently onto one of the leaves in the stream. Picturing this thought leaving your head, and settling gently onto a leaf. And then watch the thought make its way downstream.

And just this practice: if you notice more thoughts entering your mind, observe them, and then allow them to float down onto a leaf, and let them go.

You might experience having many thoughts all at once: that's ok. Sometimes minds are very busy. If this is happening, **bring your focus back** to the idea of you sitting beside the stream, and cast the thoughts outside of your mind, watching them settle in a group onto the leaves. And let the leaves carry them away.

Some thoughts might be sticky, they won't want to leave. That's ok too. If this happens, do your best to rest the thoughts outside your mind, letting them hang loosely in the air. Observe them kindly, gently. They are just thoughts, just trying to get your attention. Very kindly, allow them to

fall onto the leaves. And watch them go.

You might not have many thoughts at all. Sometimes this can happen... whatever is happening is alright. If this is the case, just focus on the picture of you, and the stream, and watch the leaves on the water. Feeling peaceful.

As you practice this exercise, you might become distracted by a thought, and run off with it. This happens all of the time. Getting our attention is what our minds do: **it's normal, and ok.** If you do notice that you've become distracted by a thought, and drifted off, just come gently back to the picture of the stream. And very kindly, and openly, let go of the thought that had your attention. And let it go...drifting away on a leaf...

Just noticing thoughts... just noticing, and putting them on leaves, and letting them go... all with a very gentle and kind attitude of awareness.

Our minds are almost always busy with thoughts, they are rarely quiet.

Some thoughts might come back, that's ok. Certain thoughts like to do that. Just notice them for what they are... **returning thoughts.** These are just thoughts. And gently letting them go, and putting them onto the leaves...

And as you are practising this focus, become aware of the stream of your thinking mind. The endless, changing shifting contents of your thoughts. Thoughts always coming, thoughts always leaving...

This is the nature of the mind. It is a constant flow of thoughts. We cannot control what shows up. But we can **control how we direct our attention.** We can control if we decide to get hooked into a thought. And we can always choose to let them go.

And now coming away from the image of you and the stream. Back into a focus on your breath, as it enters and leaves your body. Know that the stream is always here for you, always available. All you need to do to be here again is to focus.

And when you are ready, allowing your eyes to open. Bringing the idea of the leaves on the stream into the rest of your day.

How Was That For You?

I hope that you found that the leaves on a stream meditation helped you to notice and let go of your thoughts. Many of my clients find this exercise **profoundly relaxing.** It's nice to separate yourself from your thoughts in this way.

If you found that you had a little trouble visualising the stream, that's OK. You might want to **play around with visuals that work for you.** Some people use clouds across the sky rather than leaves on a stream. Some clients like to use balloons which they let go. There are no rules as to what the image is: if it works for you to notice and let go of thoughts, go for it!

If you found it difficult to let go of the thoughts, or if you **struggled** with a lot of judgemental thoughts during the exercise, that's ok too. It's a very different skill that we're trying here. Allow it to take time, and keep practising. If it stays hard, you might benefit from going to see a therapist who uses this type of mindfulness to help you troubleshoot.

It's nice to separate yourself from your thoughts in this way.

Using Letting Go Of Thoughts In Everyday Life

The best part of learning the skill of letting go of thoughts is that it is easy to put this into practice in your day to day. Once you have the idea or concept in your head of the leaves on a stream, use the phrase to prompt you when you need it.

Cynthia came to therapy when her life seemed full of conflicts. Her family were arguing with her husband's family, and as they were both from large families (and step families!), the politics were rife. Cynthia felt stuck in the middle of everybody's opinions, and was very upset and preoccupied with thoughts about what this was doing to her previously harmonious relationships.

We discussed and practised the leaves on a stream, and she loved it.

Cynthia experienced a sense of peace and was able to let go of several of her family members' attitudes. When she came back for another session she reported how much this concept had helped her out. "I was trying to get to sleep and my mind started thinking about my mother in law again, and how awful she was being to my step mother. When I noticed myself starting to worry like this, I remembered the stream and the leaf. I put my mother in law on the leaf and watched her float! The whole picture was actually kind of funny, and I noticed that I was laughing instead of crying about it. Now I just say to myself 'put it on the leaf'... when I start to get caught up".

"Put it on the leaf"

"Let it go"

CHAPTER SEVEN:

TAKING IT DEEPER:

Compassionate Mindfulness of Your Feelings

Our thoughts don't happen in isolation: whatever we think causes an emotional reaction. **Our feelings are the emotional responses to our thoughts.** For example, "I'm so sick of people asking me to do things!" is a thought, and "frustrated" is the emotional response to the thought.

Stuck as we are in our tree, we don't tend to take the time to separate our thinking from our feelings. But understanding the difference between the two, and developing skills to manage both thoughts and feelings, is extremely useful.

Most of us are never explicitly taught how to **cope with our feelings.** We learn how to deal with being emotional by observing the people around us. So if we're born into a family where everyone is fairly emotionally contained, we might pick up that the way to cope with a feeling is to 'stuff it' away inside, and not express it. If we are part of a family that likes to express their emotions, we might learn to shout and scream when we're angry or upset. Whatever we have picked up, that's ok – there's no 'right' or 'wrong' here (it's not your fault, remember?). But just noticing what you may have learned is important. How do people in your family experience and communicate their emotions? Do you tend to mirror this, or have you found your own way?

As human beings, we are emotional. We can experience **hundreds of different emotions every day.** If we're in our tree, we can become stuck, at the mercy of our emotional storms. Without compassionate awareness of feelings we run the risk of being slaves to our **emotional climate**. But by learning compassion based mindfulness, we can learn to manage our feelings in a much more useful way. I think of our feelings like a horse; and at the beginning of therapy, people's emotional horses are riding them! Compassionate mindfulness can help us to 'break the horse in', so that we are in charge, and can even get to enjoy the ride more.

The first step in dealing with our feelings is to *notice that we're having one*. This might seem very obvious, but awareness – seeing our emotional landscape – is not something we're used to doing. Similar to seeing our thoughts, becoming aware of our feelings is essential to compassionate mindful awareness.

How do we tell if we're having feelings? In some ways, **becoming aware of feelings is a little easier** than becoming aware of thoughts, because by their nature, feelings are giving us an emotional response. Emotional responses by their nature demand our attention. In evolutionary terms, our feelings have developed in order to motivate us to act, so that our needs are met. So, for example, the feeling of lonely drives us to seek company. The feeling of fear drives us to seek safety.

Tuning into our emotional lives may not be familiar just yet, but it's not difficult.

Here are some questions you might want to ask yourself:

◆ How am I feeling right now?
◆ Where in my body am I feeling this?
◆ How strong is this feeling?
◆ What name best suits this feeling? (scared, sad, angry...)

Naming the feeling – **giving it a label** – really helps to manage it. One experiment asked people to watch a stressful scene. Half of them were asked to simply notice their emotional response and to silently label it, the other half were just asked to watch it. The people who noticed and labelled their emotions experienced much less arousal in their brains, meaning that they felt less stressed.

Some of us find it very difficult to label feelings. If that's the case for you, that's ok. There is a list of emotion names in the back of this chapter, which might help you to identify what it going on for you. But if the best you can do is attach a general term – like "uncomfortable" - then that's wonderful. The important part is that you are doing your best to understand what's going on for you.

ACCEPTING FEELINGS

Once you have noticed and done your best to label the emotion, the next step is – you guessed it – accept it! Now this is truly a difficult thing to do – after all, if an unpleasant emotion arrives, most of us want it to go away, and quickly!

We tend to want the nice, pleasant feelings to stay, and **the unpleasant or difficult feelings to go away.** But like thoughts, not accepting our feelings has negative consequences. The more we demand our unpleasant feelings to leave, the more they stay, and the longer they last.

Imagine the feeling "afraid" walked in through your front door. Our automatic reaction might be to push back against the fear, and try to shove it out the door. What happens then? Two things: one, the fear pushes back (gets stronger), and two, you are locked into a struggle with fear, meaning that all of your attention is caught up in this battle. You can't do anything else while you're trying so hard to not have this feeling be here.

Acceptance of our feelings looks like this: fear shows up, walking through your front door, and you look at it, acknowledge it, and allow it to settle in your lounge room.

If we **accept and allow all of our emotions** – pleasant, unpleasant, and in-between – to be here, then we **free up a lot of our energy** to devote to other things. We don't have to spend time feeling hung up on bad feelings being around. The unpleasant feelings certainly aren't fun, but struggling with their existence doesn't do us any good. They're still here.

Let's face it: unpleasant feelings are part of life, just like unpleasant people. Most of us know and accept that we will know people whom we don't particularly like. These people might be colleagues, spouses of our friends, family members, or others who we meet in the course of our lives. And we tend to be (mostly) OK with people we don't like existing. This is because we have come to **accept** that there will be people in our lives we don't like. We know that this can happen.

To cope with people we don't like, we try our best to *tolerate* them: we don't pay them too much attention, and we may even try to spend as little time with them as possible. This is the key to acceptance of our own internal unpleasant feelings. **Treat our feelings as if they were people we don't like:** accept that they are there, try not to focus on them too much, and know that time spent with them will pass soon enough.

Here are some phrases to use that can help with acceptance: of feelings:

◆ It's ok that I am feeling
_____ right now
◆ I don't love this feeling, but I can tolerate it
◆ This feeling is here right now & I am ok with that
◆ I know I am capable of getting through this feeling

EMOTIONS ARE TEMPORARY

If we look once again at the tree, we can see that feelings are like clouds appearing in the sky. Viewing our emotional states as similar to the weather reminds us that **like the weather, they pass:** all feelings are temporary. Even people who are in the grips of extreme grief describe being hit by emotions like 'waves', which peak and trough. If we practice acceptance of our emotions, we can agree to simply be willing to sit through them, experience them and honour them.

Think about your day yesterday: how many emotions do you recall having? It is likely that there were many that arrived, stayed a little while, and then left again. This is how our feelings operate. Remembering that feelings don't last forever can be **immensely comforting** when your emotional weather turns stormy.

BEING KIND

The other day, I found my seven year old daughter crying in her bedroom. She told me that she was feeling confused about two of her little friends, who were telling her that she had to choose which of them she was going to be friends with, and that she wasn't allowed to be both of their 'best friends'. I did what came naturally – I had an overwhelming desire to **comfort** her, to put my arms around her and soothe her distress. This is kindness.

When it comes to other people, we tend to be pretty good at responding to pain. If someone we care about is upset, we notice this, and we try to comfort them. This is **empathy,** and it's a very useful skill to have. Empathy is a powerful way to form strong social bonds, giving us a sense of connection to other people. Connection is excellent for psychological and physical health – those with strong social bonds tend to be better protected from mental health problems, and even enjoy better physical health than people who are more isolated.

Unfortunately, this empathy we have for other people's emotional pain is rarely extended towards us. We are not as kind towards ourselves when we're having difficult emotions. We tend to judge our difficult emotions, to be impatient with ourselves in moments of pain. We might not even **recognise what we're going through as pain,** but view it as a weakness or something to be fixed as soon as possible.

Alison was struggling with her body image. She really hated the weight she had gained since having her second child, and most of the time her thoughts were consumed with body hatred. This was causing an immense emotional response of shame, sadness,

We are not as kind towards ourselves when we're having difficult emotions.

and desperation. But Alison did not label her emotional turmoil as pain or suffering – she simply focussed on her 'failings'. When we really looked, it was apparent that the terribly cruel things her thoughts were saying about her body were causing her to feel very painful emotions. Once Alison was able to label her feelings as pain, as suffering, she found that she started to **relate to herself** in a different way.

Kindness soothes our pain. At the heart of kindness is the desire for an end to the person's suffering, a desire for the person's wellbeing. Even if it is not possible to take someone's pain away, the intention is to reduce the intensity of the suffering and to be there for the person.

Central to developing kindfulness is the ability to **relate to your emotional life with kindness and empathy.** This might feel very foreign, but with a little practice you will see the benefit. The good part is, we already have the ability to be kind – we simply reserve it for others. Tapping into our innate kindness and directing it towards ourselves is what we are aiming for.

LOOKING AFTER FEELINGS

The meditation opposite has been designed to help you turn towards and look after difficult feelings. I would like to credit Kristen Neff, author of Self Compassion and leading researcher in this area, for pioneering this meditative practice. It can be very helpful to **teach yourself this skill,** using various difficult feelings that you actually experience during your day. At first, please make sure that you use negative situations or feelings that are not too overwhelming. Start with being frustrated with a colleague, don't start with grief or trauma. Once you feel that you're getting more of an idea of how it works, you can open up to working with more difficult feelings.

Feel free to record yourself reading this script (using your phone), and then play it back to yourself. If you would prefer to hear my voice guiding

Other kindness phrases may include:

- ◆ I'm in a really difficult place right now
- ◆ This is pain, not failure
- ◆ I'm sorry I'm feeling so bad right now
- ◆ This is really hard...I love you

you through this meditation, you can download it on itunes using this link: http://itunes.apple.com/album/id1035680975?ls=1&app=itunes

Soften, Soothe & Allow

Take some time and make sure that you have about 15-20 minutes of uninterrupted quiet. Letting yourself sit or lie in a comfortable position, making sure that your whole body is feeling supported and relaxed. And now taking a few deep breaths to help you come into this moment. And letting your breath return to normal. Not trying to change the breath at all, just being with it in its own natural rhythm.

Now call to mind a difficult situation that has happened recently in your life. Today we're going to work with difficult feelings, so it's necessary to bring up some unpleasant feelings so that we can learn how to **look after** them. Choose a situation that has been difficult but not too overwhelming. Something that brings up a level of pain that you are willing to experience and work with today. It needs to be hard but not too overwhelming or consuming.

So now that you have decided, go over the situation. What happened? Who said what? How you reacted....

See if you can understand what it is about this situation that troubled you so much. What has caused you so much pain? What is difficult about this for you?

And as you think about the situation you'll experience feelings come up. There may be more than one... see if you can give them a name. Label each of the feelings as they arrive. Trying your best to **stay open to the emotions as they come up,** and to simply, kindly name them to yourself.

Now let's see if it's possible to name the emotion that is coming up the most strongly. The one that's hurting the most, having the biggest impact. In your mind, repeat the name of this feeling a few times. And now expand your awareness and focus towards your body. See where in your body this feeling is sitting. Where in your body are you feeling this emotion? If you can feel it in a few places, focus on the place that it is present most strongly.

Then try to describe this body sensation to yourself. Is it hot, cold, heavy, constricting, dull, sharp... stay open to this physical experience. Now do your best to **soften** into that place in the body where the emotion is. Often our feelings are held in the body with tension. See if it is possible for you to relax around it.

It might be possible for you to explore around the edges of where this emotion is, and try to direct an idea of softening there. As if you were visiting the boundary of that feeling, and trying to soften or blur the boundary. You might want to repeat in your mind the word soften... soften... soften...

Now we'll try to actually look after you as you are experiencing this emotion.

Feeling like this is difficult, it hurts. Try to **direct the idea of soothing** towards this place in your body. Of doing your best to look after it. It might help to put your hand on the place in the body where you're feeling the emotion, or maybe to put your hand on your heart to connect you with a sense of soothing. You might have some kind words for yourself at this moment. Words like, it's ok... or I'm so sorry this is happening for you...or even repeat the word... soothing.... soothing... soothing....

If this gets overwhelming at any time, go back to the focus on your breath, and anchor there for a little while, until you feel ready to face the feelings again. There is no rush...

Now let's see if we can just let the feeling be here. You are not trying to make this feeling go away. It's just noticing, just softening... soothing... see if you can let go of the desire for this feeling to be gone. Let this be as it will, let it happen as it will.

You might want to **think of this feeling as a visitor to your body.** See if you can just let it be here, knowing that it won't stay forever. If it feels ok you might want to repeat the word allow... allow... allow...

Often our feelings are held in the body with tension.

If you notice your mind wandering during this practice, that's OK. Just notice, and gently bring it back to the attention on the feeling.

And you might notice the feeling changing, becoming a different feeling. If that happens that's ok. Just repeat the process of trying to **label the emotion,** find it in your body, describe it to yourself... soften, soothe... and allow...

Just soften... soothe... allow... And now coming back to the awareness of your breath as it enters and leaves your body. Coming away from the focus on the feeling. And gently opening your eyes.

How Was That For You?

This is a very powerful exercise, and can be quite confronting. Many of us are just not used to facing difficult feelings and staying with them. If you found that it was quite hard, that's OK. Congratulate yourself for **being brave** enough to give it a go.

If you are finding this terribly overwhelming and hard to manage, I would gently advise you to find someone to help you – a great therapist. You don't need to do this on your own.

People generally find this meditation to help deal with their feelings. With practice, it can become easier to notice and allow feelings to arrive in your life, without getting engulfed or overwhelmed by them.

LOOKING AFTER OUR FEELINGS: SUMMARY

When stormy feelings hit, here's a quick way of remembering what to do:
1. Notice that you're having a feeling
2. Give it a label/name (I am feeling _____ right now)
3. Accept the feeling (It is ok that I am feeling _____ right now)
4. Be with the feeling – sit with it, knowing that it will not last forever
5. Be kind to yourself, soothe yourself
6. Once the feeling has passed, congratulate yourself for making the effort to take care of you in a difficult time

A MANTRA FOR VERY DIFFICULT FEELINGS

This is a self-compassion practice from Kristen Neff, a leading researcher and mother to a severely autistic child.

In particularly challenging times, it can be useful to repeat the following words to yourself:

◆ This is a moment of pain
◆ Pain is a part of life
◆ I wish myself peace

I love this mantra, because it very neatly summarises what we've been talking about. The first part 'this is a moment of pain' helps us to recognise what we're going through as a suffering, rather than a failure or a problem to be fixed. By calling it a 'moment', we remind ourselves that the intensity of this pain won't be here always, that it is temporary.

The second part, 'pain is a part of life', allows this pain to be here, it makes it ok, normal, part of our human experience. This stops us struggling with the pain and just lets it be there, without judgement. The third part, 'I wish myself peace', is a lovely way of soothing the pain, a reminder that we want to feel better. Saying the whole mantra is an act of self-care, and a wonderful, quick way of staying mindful.

I often use this mantra, for the little things (children screaming) to the big things (people dying). It works for both. When I do it, I tend to put my hand on my heart, to reinforce the soothing part at the end. I find it greatly comforting.

TOUCH

When people we love are distressed, what do we do? We'll give them a hug, or rub them on the back, or squeeze their hand. This type of response – to connect physically – is universal. But why do we do it?

It turns out there is sound science behind this very loving behaviour. When we're distressed, our stress hormones are released, in particular cortisol, widely known as the stress hormone. Cortisol makes us feel agitated and unsafe. Feelings of fear and anger are often associated with cortisol responses.

Amazingly, when we are touched by another human being (or even an animal), a cortisol antagonist hormone – oxytocin – is released into our bloodstream. Oxytocin is known as a 'caregiving' hormone. When it's released into the body, we start to feel safe, warm, cared for, and nurtured. Oxytocin is the predominant hormone released by breastfeeding women when they nurse their babies, which scientists believes helps them to attach and feel love for their babies.

So touch from another human being can really help us to calm down and stop the stress response. If you can, try to hug someone – a full body hug – for a good thirty seconds or so, and see how you start to feel.

Even more fascinating is research that shows that we don't even need it to be another person in order to produce oxytocin releases within our bodies. We can **stimulate oxytocin release,** and therefore calm ourselves down – just by touching ourselves. Isn't that amazing?

There are some specific places on the body that are especially sensitive to eliciting an oxytocin response.

You'll know if the touch is working for you if you **feel a little release of warmth.** If you don't feel it, that's ok, just persevere with the touch anyway, knowing that this soothing touch is calming down your body, even if you can't feel it.

Like the senses, some of the places that you touch might trigger a more intense oxytocin release than others.

For me, the face massage and vagus nerve produce the most vivid feelings of warmth. If you find one place is particularly powerful, then it's likely that you'll use that area as your 'go-to' in times of need.

Here's some of the ways you could try to get that response all by yourself:

- ◆ Place one of your hands on the middle of your chest. This touches your heart.
- ◆ Give yourself a head massage
- ◆ Massage your face, including the ears
- ◆ Locate the little lump at the base of your neck at the back of your head. If you run your fingers upwards from that lump up along the middle of the back of the neck, you're stimulating the vagus nerve.
- ◆ The vagus nerve is chock full of oxytocin.
- ◆ Giving yourself a little mini-hug by wrapping your arms around your own waist can mimic being hugged by others and makes you feel secure, reassured.
- ◆ Holding your own hand can also trigger an oxytocin release.

EMOTIONS

accepting
admiration
adoration
affection
afraid
agitated
agreeable
aggressive
agony
alarmed
alienated
amazed
amused
angry
anguish
annoyed
anticipating
anxious
apprehensive
aroused
assertive
assured
astonished
attached
attracted
awed
beleaguered
bewitched
bitter
bliss
blue

bored
calculating
calm
capricious
caring
cautious
charmed
cheerful
closeness
compassion
complacent
compliant
composed
contempt
conceited
concerned
content
crabby
crazed
cross
cruel
defeated
defiant
delighted
dependant
depressed
desire
disappointed
disapproval
discontent
disenchanted

disgust
disillusioned
dislike
dismay
displeasure
dissatisfied
distracted
distressed
disturbed
doubtful
dread
eager
earnest
easy-going
ecstatic
elated
embarrassed
enamored
enchanted
enjoyment
enraged
enraptured
enthralled
enthusiastic
envious
equanimity
euphoria
exasperated
excited
exhausted
extroverted

exuberant
fascinated
fatalistic
fearful
ferocious
fierce
flummoxed
flustered
fond
fright
frustrated
furious
generous
glad
gloating
gloomy
glum
greedy
grief
grim
grouchy
grumpy
guilt
happy
harried
homesick
hopeless
horror
hostile
humiliated
hurt

hysterical
infatuated
inferior
insecure
insulted
interested
introverted
irritated
isolated
jaded
jealous
jittery
jolly
jovial
joyful
jubilant
judged
keen
kindly
laid back
lazy
loathing
lonely
longing
love
lulled
lust
mad
merry
miserable
modest

mortified
naughty
needy
neglected
nervous
open
optimistic
outgoing
outraged
panic
passion
passive
peaceful
pensive
pessimistic
pity
placid
pleased
proud
pushy
quarrelsome
queasy
quiet
rage
rapture
reflective
rejected
relief
remorse
repentance
resentment

resigned
revulsion
roused
sadness
sarcastic
sardonic
satisfaction
scared
scorn
self-assured
self-
congratulatory
self-satisfied
sentimental
serene
shame
sheepish
shocked
silly
smug
sorrow
sorry
spellbound
spite
stingy
stoic
stressed
subdued
submissive
suffering
superior

surprise
sympathy
tenderness
tense
terror
threatened
thrilled
timid
tormented
tranquil
triumphant
trusting
uncomfortable
unhappy
unsure
upset
vain
vengeful
vexed
vigilant
vivacious
wary
watchful
weary
woeful
wondering
worried
wrathful
zesty

CHAPTER EIGHT

CULTIVATING SELF~COMPASSION

Our Inner Judge

When we take a close look at how we speak to ourselves, one thing becomes obvious: often, we're not very nice. For many of us, self-talk is peppered with nasty comments, criticisms, demands to be better, insults, put downs, and impatience. Why are we like this?

We can start to make sense of this inner meanness by taking a look at the concept of **self-esteem,** a term many of us are familiar with. In psychological terms, self-esteem refers to how we globally evaluate ourselves: how we feel about ourselves as people. These self-evaluations tend to be based upon two areas: **performance and comparison.** In a nutshell, how well we're doing in various areas of life, and how we're measuring up to other people.

So if we're doing well – good feedback at work, relationships are stable, losing weight – then we may evaluate ourselves positively, and feel 'good'.

"I'm looking pretty good right now, liking this new slimmer version of myself! And all of the comments I'm getting are great! People are jealous! I can't believe it took me this long to stop being lazy".

But of course, life doesn't always go well. We don't always win, and we're not always the best. And this is when self-esteem can let us down. When life gets hard - when our partner is cheating, when the weight returns – our self-talk turns on us, and starts to criticise, judge, and berate us. **Our inner voice -is critical,** impatient with the failure, and demands that we 'fix' things so that we can feel better again.

"I can't believe I blew it! All of this weight has come back, and it's all my own stupid fault! What's wrong with me?! So typical of stupid me to screw everything up. If I wasn't such a loser everything would be ok. I have to get back there!"

As you can see, self esteem is like a **'fair weather friend'** – it's only nice to us when things are going well. But when life is harder, and we're struggling, out come the knives! The truth is that we can't be perfect all of the time. We are human beings: we will fail, we will make mistakes, our lives will go wrong at times. And during hard times, rather than **being there for ourselves,** we judge.

We are all socialised to think of ourselves in such conditional terms. From the moment we are born, we're compared to others, spoken to about winning or losing, and encouraged to 'be the best'. It's no surprise that competitive ways of thinking show up in our thinking 'trees'. But having a relationship with ourselves that is conditional – that is, only nice if we're doing well – can be ultimately damaging.

SHAME

The Oxford dictionary defines shame as "A painful feeling of humiliation or distress caused by the consciousness of wrong or foolish behaviour". Shame is a direct result of speaking to ourselves in a harsh, judgemental, and critical way. We can **feel very alone and isolated** from other people when times get tough, especially if we are internally evaluating our experience as a 'failure'. People's weight gain, demotions, or inability to afford a holiday rarely get posted on Facebook or Instagram. Shame and feeling alone leads people to hide away from other people, and their feelings can worsen as a result of this. Shame **disconnects us** from other people and the world.

Helen was a yo-yo dieter who had lost and regained 20kg several times in her adult life. When she was performing well, being 'good' with her diet, she felt great: "I look fantastic, I can do this, look at all the attention I'm getting!" She admitted that when she was losing weight, she felt a certain level of feeling 'better-than" her sister, who experienced similar weight struggles.

But when Helen fell off the diet wagon and regained the weight, she felt terrible about herself, and became her own worst critic. "I can't believe what a total failure I am. How can I let this happen again? Why don't I learn? I'm so stupid". Helen would then make plans to lose the weight again so that she could feel better about herself as a person. Helen would also avoid her sister during such times, because she felt so "less-than" when the weight came back.

Helen's **shame spiral** was so bad that it tended to worsen her self care rather than improve it. To deal with the painful feelings of shame, Helen would comfort eat – her 'go-to' when times were hard. And of course the irony of this was, the more she comfort ate (to relieve strong feelings of shame), the more the shame would return. It was a vicious cycle that she felt very 'stuck' in.

JUDGEMENT AS A MOTIVATOR

Our harsh self judgement, of course, has a function: it's there to make you try to fix things. And underlying this command to fix things is a desire to make you feel happy with yourself. So in a sense, **even your judgement wants you to be happy** – it's just that it goes about it in a very bad way!

At a superficial level, judgement can work: many of us go through life driven by the inner judge and frantically trying to perfect ourselves all the time. But I have many clients who come because they find that **judgement just doesn't 'work' anymore.** Rather than trying to fix things, they've stopped trying altogether. And of course not trying at all increases their judgement, and their sense of shame. This is where Helen was when I met her. In spite of ruthless judgement that she was hearing most of her waking life, she wasn't taking care of herself.

Helen thought she was alone. She couldn't understand why she wasn't doing the one thing that she wanted most in the world. But from a psychological perspective, her response is perfectly normal. We know that driving ourselves with high standards and critical judgement works for a little while, but then most of us will 'freeze' and stop trying altogether. It's basic human nature – we don't keep striving and trying if we are continuously punished. This 'freeze' can last for a long time, and the irony is that when people freeze their **judgement goes into overdrive** - which just increases the freeze!

Judging yourself out of inaction won't work. Many psychologists have seen that the construct of self-esteem itself is quite unhelpful, and have cast around for alternative ways of helping people to relate to themselves in a more helpful way.

SELF-COMPASSION: GETTING OUT OF THE DEEP FREEZE

Even though judgement is our default, we can learn to become **our own best friends** rather than our own worst enemy. This is taking mindfulness to a deeper level: to one of *kindfulness*.

The concept of self-compassion has been central to Buddhism for thousands of years. In recent years, psychologists have seen the great benefit of this way of approaching oneself, and have spent time developing ways of **teaching people how to become self-compassionate.** This doesn't mean you'll become a Buddhist! The way we teach self-compassion is not in any way religious, we're just using the concepts to build skills to change your relationship with yourself.

At the centre of self-compassion models is the idea that **humans are imperfect, and flawed.** This imperfection is seen as normal and expected, something to be experienced in life.

The self-esteem concept views our human struggles – failure, mistakes, even our negative thoughts and feelings themselves – as 'flaws' that need to be changed and perfected. In contrast, the self-compassion model reframes all of these not as 'flaws' but as *struggle*. Seeing whatever we are going through as a suffering, a normal, human suffering. There's nothing 'wrong' about it, it's just pain.

Because imperfection is normal and expected, when it happens, using self-compassion we **respond to our own suffering or difficulty with kindness and warmth,** rather than judging it as an awful, shameful failure.

Think about how we approach other people who are going through difficult times. When we see another person suffering, we respond to their pain and distress with words and gestures of kindness. Phrases like "I'm so sorry you're going through this" or physical gestures, like giving someone a hug, are common ways of responding when other people are in trouble. It's something that comes effortlessly for most of us, this ability to be compassionate and kind when people we care about hit hard times.

Even though it's not what we're used to, we can learn to develop the **skill of compassion for ourselves**. Because we're used to being nice to other people, all we need to learn to do is how to direct this innate kindness towards us.

Self-compassion also **addresses the problem of feeling shame** in response to life's difficulties. In a self-esteem model, hard times and failures make us feel alone and isolated. But self-compassion includes the wonderful idea of connection in pain - that everything we can possibly go through in life is part of being human. The simple reminder that whatever we are going through, whatever emotion, situation or experience we are encountering, it is part of human experience: someone else has been through this – you are not alone. This is **deeply powerful** to combat the shame that many people feel when they are wrestling with self-esteem based judgement.

Helen felt alone in her diet 'failure', and the urge to hide her shame by withdrawing from her sister. By mentally bringing up the idea of human

connection, Helen reminded herself that although this was a difficult time, many thousands of humans had been through this experience of weight regain. She was even able to see that her own sister had experienced weight regain struggles. This way of thinking made Helen more able to **feel connected and close** to her sister – and to the world - rather than feeling ashamed and withdrawing.

Many of my clients breathe a sigh of relief when we have this conversation about the normality of suffering. It's almost as if they are suddenly given permission to be human, to be imperfect, and to accept that things won't always be easy.

HOW TO DEVELOP SELF-COMPASSION

Self-compassion involves three basic steps:
1. Noticing whatever you're going through and seeing it as a suffering rather than a 'failure' or 'problem' to be fixed
2. Responding to your own suffering with kindness and empathy rather than judgement
3. Connecting with the humanity of your experience

Here's a guide to training yourself to become more self-compassionate in your day to day life:

Step 1: Noticing
If you are ''failing' at something, get into the habit of re-labelling it as a hardship. Use the idea of "Getting into the sun" - pull back from your thoughts and feelings, see what it is you're experiencing, and notice how it makes you feel.

For example, today I need to send an email to someone, and I have to tell her something that I know she won't like. And to be honest, I'm procrastinating!

I can hear my voice of judgement saying something like this:

"Come on, stop being so rude to her, you're so gutless! You should have done this days ago. A fine mess you're making, avoiding the issue. What kind of psychologist are you!"

So now I'm going to just notice this moment, *as a suffering*, instead of buying into the thoughts that there's something wrong with me for avoiding this:

"I can see these thoughts, thoughts of judgement about how I'm handling the situation... I can also see my pain – this is hard for me, to confront someone, to say something negative which might hurt their feelings. **This is my pain, this is my struggle**".

Can you see the difference between the two? I'm getting a different perspective, by pulling out of the judgement and seeing it objectively, as it is, and by reframing it as struggle, I am able to feel a little more empathy towards myself.

Step 2: Being Kind
The next step is to respond to your struggle with kindness. With warmth. An easy way to get started with being kind is to imagine a friend or someone in your own life who makes you feel effortlessly compassionate. Someone you dearly care for, and would do anything to help. This might be a child, or a dear friend. It might be someone in your distant past, or even someone you don't know but who brings up that warm sense of compassion and

unconditional love. Do you have someone in mind?

Once you do, imagine that the suffering that you are experiencing right now had happened to them. Imagine that they have just told you their story, and you have heard it compassionately. Ask yourself, **what would you say to them?**

What would you say to someone you truly loved, in that moment?

If I conjure up my compassionate friend (my best friend Jo, whom I absolutely adore), and imagine that she had just told me about her procrastination, and how annoyed she was with herself for it, I come up with this:

"Oh, it's OK! Don't beat yourself up, it's so hard to face these things sometimes…it's hard to confront people. I think it's brave that you're going to do it, and it's absolutely normal that you don't want to do it! I know you're strong enough to do this, even if it scares you".

Can you see how much this changes things? I just went from feeling totally ashamed about dodging the email to **feeling totally supported in my feelings of fear.**

Step 3: Connection

The final step in developing self-compassion in your everyday life is to mentally connect with the humanity of whatever you're going through. So using my example, I'm remembering how many people in my life avoid confronting people with negative feedback. And extending this idea even further in my head, to imagining the hundreds of thousands of humans, all of us feeling afraid sometimes to speak up, in case we get rejected… it's so **very, very human and fragile** to be like this. I feel included in this mass of frail, imperfect humanity, rather than feeling locked out of normality. It's wonderfully inclusive!

And you know what? I just sent the email….

So here's a cheat sheet for using compassion in your everyday life:
1. Notice
2. Be Kind
3. Connect

We can learn to develop the skill of compassion for ourselves.

A SELF-COMPASSION MEDITATION

Many of my clients 'understand' the concept of self-compassion on an intellectual level, but say that they struggle to **really feel, or believe it.** This is fairly normal. To help you to take the idea from an intellectual level to more of a felt sense, self-compassion meditation is wonderful. I have included my favourite self-compassion meditation below. I encourage you to give it a go, and see how it feels.

Feel free to record yourself reading this script (using your phone), and then play it back to yourself. If you would prefer to hear my voice guiding you through this meditation, you can download it on itunes using this link: http://itunes.apple.com/album/id1035680975?ls=1&app=itunes

The Compassionate Friend

Sitting or lying down, making sure that you are in a very comfortable position. Gently closing your eyes. Take a few deep breaths to calm yourself. Noticing how your lungs feel as you breathe in, and out. And now letting your breathing find its own natural rhythm, not trying to force it or change it in any way. Just be with your breath.

Imagine yourself now in a room that feels very safe... **cosy, and comfortable.** This is your idea of the most perfect room imaginable, it's just exactly the way you like it. Imagine what the room would look like. The furniture... the lighting. Imagine yourself sitting or lying in this room, making yourself very comfortable.

You'll soon receive a visitor to this safe room of yours. A being of light, who embodies a sense of deep, bottomless, unconditional love and acceptance. **A being of warmth, compassion, and great wisdom.**

Let yourself receive the gaze of this endlessly loving, compassionate creature.

This being might be a deity figure like Christ or Buddha. Or it might be a compassionate person from your life, past or present. It could even be a beloved pet. A character from a movie or book. This being may not even have a physical form, it could be just a presence of light and warmth, with no body to speak of. Whatever image comes up for you, ensure that this being is the ultimate in **unconditional love and compassion.** This being wants to visit with you for a while... it wants to be your friend.

Your room has a door in it which you can go to, and open. Please go to the door to let your compassionate companion in. Settling now back inside your room with your compassionate friend. Placing yourself with them in a way that feels right for you...sitting next

to them, holding hands, they may even be in your lap. There's no right way to be, except what feels good. **Allow yourself** now to simply be seen by this being. Let yourself receive the gaze of this endlessly loving, compassionate creature. Feel the warmth, unconditional acceptance of you from them. Allow yourself to feel how deeply you are loved by them. Know that you don't have to do anything. **Just to be, and to be seen.** Enjoy the feelings of absolute acceptance and openness. Just enjoy the company of this being.

Your compassionate friend wants to tell you something now...something that's just what you need to hear right now in your life. Listen carefully to what they are saying. And if no words come, that's OK too. Just enjoy being held in their loving presence.

Perhaps there is something you would like to say...if so feel free. And allow them to respond if they choose too...if they don't that's OK.

Listening deeply... is there anything else? Your compassionate friend wants to give you something now. A material object. Open your hands and **let yourself receive the gift.** Be open to whatever it is. This has a special meaning just for you, right now in your life. Study it carefully. Feel the loving intention that underlies this gift. What does it mean for you?

Allowing yourself to be held once again in the warmth of the gaze of your compassionate friend. Knowing that now it is time for your friend to go, but know also that they can come back whenever you like. Walking your friend to the door of the room, and exchange a final, loving glance. Feel the bottomless care from this being towards you. Feel the desire for your own wellbeing from this being.

And saying farewell, close the door. You are now once again alone in your room. Let yourself **savour what just happened.** Enjoy the memory of the gaze, words, the object that you still hold in your hands. Notice any feelings that you are experiencing, and be open to them. Sit with them, whatever they are.

Now it is time for you to leave your room, knowing that **you can return whenever you wish.** All you need to do to be here again is to focus.

Coming away from the picture of your room, and back into an awareness of your breath as it enters and leaves your body. And when you are ready, gently opening your eyes and coming back to the present.

How Was That For You?

A lot of people find the compassionate friend exercise very powerful. To really *feel* compassion directed towards yourself is very different to simply **understanding at a logical level that being kind is useful.** I hope that you were able to receive the felt sense of unconditional love and acceptance.

If nothing much happened for you during the meditation, that's ok. People have very complicated reactions to self-compassion, and if you're one of them, that's ok. Allow it to be complicated, and take some time to understand how your mind is reacting to it. Keep trying the practice and see what shows up. And of course if you're really struggling, find a therapist who specialises in self-compassion.

Please 'dip in' to self-compassion regularly during your life. Visit your special room and **meet with your compassionate friend on a regular basis.** You might find that the room changes, that the compassionate friend changes, the words or the objects given change. All of this is ok and normal.

WILL BEING SELF-COMPASSIONATE MAKE ME A COUCH POTATO?

When I speak to people about self-compassion, often they are concerned that it sounds **'indulgent'**, or that being nice to themselves will 'let them off the hook' in some way. People fear that they will stop striving, stop trying to go after their goals. This goes back to that old belief we have that judgement will somehow motivate us to strive and achieve.

At its heart, compassion is a desire for the wellbeing of another. Self-compassion, then, is the **desire for our own wellbeing.** If we really want the best for ourselves, we will not become self-indulgent.

I have infinite compassion towards my three year old daughter, but I don't give in to her every whim. If she had it her way, she would never brush her teeth. But because I have her wellbeing in mind, I make her do it!

So I hope you can see that self-compassion and kindness are far from self-indulgence. Sometimes being kind to yourself means putting in an effort, or getting out of your **comfort zone.** It's not just about doing what you feel like doing right now, it's about sticking with what's best for you in the big picture. Right now as I write, I am being tempted to not go for my afternoon run. There's a part of me that is feeling sleepy and unenthused. But if I tap into my compassion, and ask myself – what would be good for me right now? - I can see that heading out the door & having that run will make me feel better later. So, off I go...

What is good for me right now?
What do I really need?

Listening deeply... is there anything else?

WHAT ABOUT THE JUDGEMENT?

As you practice being more self-compassionate, you'll notice that **the voice of judgement still happens.** This is normal – your judgemental self-talk is very automatic, it's 'hard-wired', very old neural pathways operate to make the thoughts occur even when we don't want them too. The aim of self-compassion isn't to make the judgement go away completely: it may never totally vanish. But the more you practice developing a compassionate voice, the stronger that voice will become. It's like a muscle: imagine your right arm is the strong, old bicep muscle that you've been flexing every day for years. It's huge!

And on your left arm, there's a tiny little bicep muscle which you don't use nearly as often. But with a conscious effort to practice, little by little, this muscle will grow. So please, continue to try to speak to yourself in a more compassionate way, and with time, it will become **more automatic and feel less awkward.**

Self Compassion Written Practice

Some of my clients find it useful to do some writing practice to help 'cement' a more compassionate voice inside their heads. This involves taking time to notice whenever your inner judge is speaking to you, and jotting it down on a piece of paper or in a journal. Then, when you have some time to reflect, write down a **'compassionate response'** to the judgemental thought. Here's an example:

Judgement Says	Compassion Says ("What would I say to someone I dearly loved who was saying this to themselves?")
You're such a loser for forgetting to pay that bill. What kind of responsible adult does that?! You never get anything right.	Hey, don't be so mean to yourself. You've got a lot on your plate and it's understandable that this slipped your mind. You're doing the best you can. How can you look after your stress levels today?
No-one has responded to your texts all day because they don't like you. You're boring and ugly.	Woah that's not ok to talk to me like that! I am a wonderful person and people love me. I love me! This bully voice needs to pull its head in!

When you're starting out, accessing a more compassionate response might be very difficult. This is because the judgement voice is so loud – it's a 'default', familiar and often very loud voice! Even if this is so, practising **the voice of compassion** is important.

At first, it doesn't need to be loud. You don't even need to believe it. Just practice writing down something compassionate, and gradually this habit of being more supportive towards yourself will grow.

The more you practice developing a compassionate voice, the stronger that voice will become.

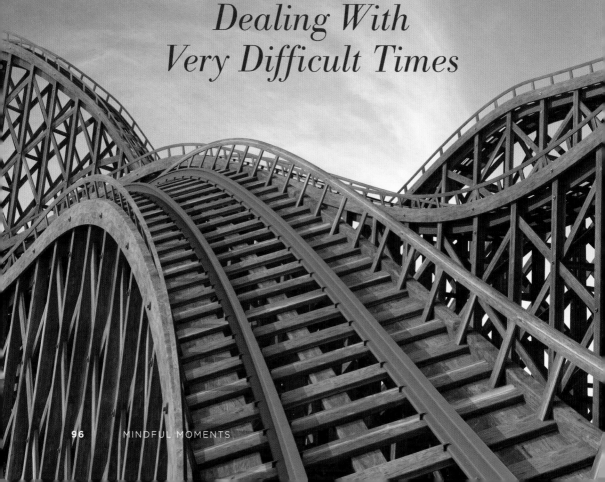

CHAPTER NINE

NAVIGATING LIFE'S UPS *and* DOWNS:

Dealing With Very Difficult Times

Life is full of pain, and as we have seen, compassionate mindfulness skills can be very helpful in helping us manage painful feelings. But what about times when life is really, truly difficult? What about times of great tragedy, of loss? In a nutshell, what do we do **when life truly sucks?**

Very few of us get through life scott free: most of us will suffer. There may be great loss, such as the death of a family member. Or horrible injustice: you may become a victim of a terrible crime. You might be faced with a life-threatening or even terminal illness. When things like this pop up, **we're rarely prepared** for it. And it can seem impossible to imagine that we'd be able to cope.

But there are steps you can take to help yourself through such times. At first, a common human response to the event is to fight with it – to struggle. To not accept that this thing could happen. To say to yourself at a very deep level that this can't be happening.

"No!...they can't be dead!"

"What do you mean I've got cancer? I'm too young?!"

This is extremely common when we initially hear bad news. And it can take a while to sink in: sometimes people even forget that this terrible thing has happened. We wake up in the morning, and for a minute or two, everything is ok – and then we remember. **And we don't want it.** It's as if the experience we're going through is so far removed from our normal every day that it doesn't 'fit' anywhere in our minds. Like waking up to a living nightmare.

ACCEPTANCE

One of the first skills to embrace is acceptance: agreeing that this thing can happen in your life. Even if you don't want it to be happening. Even if it's your worst nightmare. It can happen. This is part of it.

At first, **acceptance talk can seem bizarre,** because we don't want to believe it. But working on allowing this event to have happened is important, to reduce the risk of 'Level 2 judgement'. Struggle, and judgement, can intensify our pain, because on some level we're telling ourselves that this pain is unacceptable. Which doesn't remove the pain, it just removes our permission to experience it!

KINDNESS

Kindness is very needed during awful times. But this might be the point at which our default judgement comes up strongly: this is because it's old, hardwired, and reflexive. Not because it's true. Do your best to **treat yourself with great kindness at this time,**

bottomless, endless care and concern concentrated towards you. Practice the compassionate friend exercise if you feel up to it. Be kind.

CONNECTION

When horrific things happen to us, it's easy to feel alone, isolated. To feel like the only one going through it. If you have cancer, you might walk down the street looking at healthy people, feeling different. If your husband has left you, you can feel like the only single parent in the world. If you've just lost your mother, you look around and suddenly see people with their mothers everywhere. It's easy to feel different, suddenly isolated in your pain. But something to try is this **idea of connection in human experience:** whatever you are going through right now, it is part of being human. Many people have gone through this before, and will continue to go through this. You are **not alone** in this experience: you are part of a life experience that happens to people. In this sense, because it's part of being alive, it's *ok* that this is happening.

For every intact family you see on the street, there exists a family who are not intact. If you see a person enjoying time with their mother, know that there are many people out there without a mother. If you see people that you think are healthy, know that cancer has touched their lives as well. Whatever you are going through, no matter how horrific, it is part of the human condition.

FINDING MEANING

We have talked about coping with uncomfortable feelings, and how remembering that they are temporary can be a way of finding willingness to sit with them and look after them.

Now of course, when terrible things happen in your life, they are not 'temporary'. They are life-changing events. This can be very challenging to accept: that this might change you, in a big way, for a long time – perhaps even for the rest of your life. If the event isn't something we bargained for, this is a tremendously bitter pill to swallow.

When people come for help at terrible times in their lives, they want to know how long it will be until the pain will go away. They want to 'deal' with it, fix it, with the hope that at some point they can go back to how things were before the terrible change. This is so understandable: this urge to go back to a time of innocence, to a life in which this pain isn't happening.

I think of big, painful events like this in a different way. Our minds are like a

room, and inside the room is us. There's furniture in the room, which represents the big things that define us: people and relationships, our professions, our passions, memories. When something big happens, it's like a new piece of furniture is delivered to our room. We don't want to accept delivery of it, but like it or not, it's here. So the process of 'dealing' with this event isn't about waiting for this bit of furniture to go away. It's about making space for it in your room. Finding a place for it to fit. And eventually, getting used to it.

Your room – your mind, your life – might never be the same. But that's ok. **That's as it should be.** If you didn't have such a huge response to the event, you wouldn't be human. You may experience some grief and sadness related to this realisation: this is normal. Allow the sadness to come as you let go of the idea that things might not be the same again.

If the event has been a death or the loss of someone very close to you, the idea of the piece of furniture can be **strangely comforting.** Although this person is gone, they are here, inside your head. In my head, my mother is a comfortable arm chair. When I want to feel close to her, I go and sit in that chair, and let the memories – and the sadness – come.

If the event is terrifying, frightening, or traumatic, the idea of this piece of furniture moving in forever is not at all comforting. But again, we have no choice in this furniture being here: it's just here. So we can look at the idea of finding the meaning in the pain. This is different for everyone, and there's **no right or wrong way to approach it.**

Research has shown that people who go through difficult times are often much more resilient than people who haven't had such experiences. They can be very 'wise' and often much more appreciative of life, of the simple things. If we have experienced great fear, horrible terror, we can develop a much more **enriched appreciation for the everyday things,** like the sun shining in the sky or just walking down the street.

Allow the sadness to come as you let go of the idea that things might not be the same again.

As a psychologist I am privileged enough to witness people's stories, to hear countless tales of loss, terror, and pain. **I'm awestruck by how much we can bear,** how much we can take, and how people come to terms with these events. I often ask people "what has this event taught you?" "What has it shown you?"

Alex is thirty and has survived two different types of cancer. Her meaning is this - "it's shown me to appreciate every day as much as I can, to speak my mind, and to love people deeply". Lorna, another of my clients was the victim of a pack rape, and she almost didn't survive the ordeal. After many months of coming to terms with the fear that this piece of furniture brought, she was able to start exploring the meaning of the pain. Very simply, it was this: "courage". When she looked at that piece of furniture in her mind, she was able to connect with the reality that she had **survived the worst thing possible, and she was still here.** And that she was the bravest person she knew. This made her fear much less, and she was able to live.

Once that question is explored with a sense of acceptance and curiosity, people are able to find the meaning. Once the meaning is found, that piece of furniture isn't quite so resented.

SOAKING UP THE SWEET SPOTS

We've talked about how compassionate mindfulness can help us to cope with hard, difficult, and downright horrible times in life. But compassionate mindfulness can also help us to **soak up the good stuff.** Our human brains aren't very well geared to pay attention to positive things. Our brains evolved to pay more attention to threat signals and danger than to joy and laughter, and this of course means that we are very good at surviving. But perhaps **not so automatically well equipped for thriving!**

Paying more attention to the good, the positive, and the joyful things in life is so rewarding. When we use compassionate mindfulness to get more involved with the good stuff, everyday happy events can become literally amazing.

One practice to use to help us to connect more with joyful moments is called the **'sweet spot'.** To do this, I want you to think of a moment, a memory that has happened to you, which struck you as particularly breathtaking. One of those life moments which made you want to **press 'pause'** and just stay there, taking it in.

I have two of these moments. One of them was when my oldest daughter was about three months old. Like all new mums, I was so tired all the time! It was late afternoon, and I had been breastfeeding her on the bed. I fell asleep, and so did she. A little while later I woke up. When I opened my eyes, she was right there - looking at me with her enormous blue eyes staring right at me. Our heads were close together, and I remember being physically struck by her gaze, and **the beauty and innocence took my breath away.** I can't think about that moment without getting goosebumps!

My other sweet spot moment happened when I was away for the weekend. We went for a walk to the beach very early in the morning, around sunrise. This particular weekend was a tragic one for Australia, as it was during some terrible bushfires which claimed the lives of many people. The whole mood of the weekend was affected by this huge fire and the catastrophe taking place in Victoria. We walked down towards the beach and came around the corner, and there in front of us was the most brilliant sunrise I have ever seen.

The sun was a huge ball of fire, pink, red, orange – the entire sky was on fire. The moment again, struck me and took away my ability to speak, move – I could only look, and admire.

So these are 'sweet spots' in my life – times that simply seared themselves into my brain. We all experience these moments, and as you can see they don't have to be 'big' events, **they can be small moments, but exquisite.**

The Sweet Spot exercise is all about deliberately practising remembering such moments, in all of their delightful detail. Literally closing your eyes and letting yourself relive them, immersing yourself in them. The benefits of this practice are many: they can help make you feel good if you're having a rough day. If you do this type of practice regularly, you're doing more than just making yourself feel good. You're actually changing how your brain works. Focusing on intensely positive memories will lead your brain to release calming, soothing, pleasure related hormones, literally 'soothing' your brain. You are also **developing the skill of holding onto the positive** rather than letting them fall through your awareness.

You're actually changing how your brain works.

THE SWEET SPOT

1. Jot down your own 'sweet spot' experiences. Think back to moments in your life that pop out; that strike you as particularly enjoyable, powerful, intense moments.

2. Giving yourself some time, sit down quietly and close your eyes. Begin to relive the sweet spot experience. Go step by step through it, start at the beginning. For each moment of your sweet spot, try to **connect with as many senses as you can:** what you could see, hear, smell, feel, touch, taste. Particularly connect with how the moment made you feel. Get curious as to what it was about the experience

that affected you so much. What was it that moved you?

3. Sit in the memories, replay the moment, each time immersing yourself in the feeling of being affected by the moment. Really go there. Allow emotions to come up: if you get tearful, that's ok.

4. When it feels right to step away from the sweet spot, come back. Jot down as much as you can about the experience, make your notes as vivid and a sense filled as you can. This writing practice will help you to cement the sweet spot in your mind.

The Sweet Spot is always there for you as **a way to dip into a beautiful mindfulness practice.** And in the course of your day to day life, if a sweet spot should happen, you'll be equipped to really soak it up like a sponge!

CHAPTER TEN:

LIVE THE LIFE YOU WANT:

Connecting With Meaning

We have talked a lot about using compassionate mindfulness skills to let go of unhelpful, overlearned ways of thinking. But these patterns of thinking and feeling have played an important role in our lives – they have dictated what we do. A lot of our past decisions have been made by our automatic thoughts.

So what now? How do you make decisions and know which path to take without relying on your 'default' ways of thinking?

An alternative to letting our automatic thoughts guide our lives is to **connect with our values.** Values mean what's in our heart of hearts: what we stand for and truly, genuinely believe in. Values reflect our heart's deepest desires, our core self, an authentic, *felt* sense of what's 'right' for us. A lot of people talk about 'going with their gut', and I believe that this refers to a values based decision.

We don't often take the time to think about what we really want from life. We spend so much time attached to our chattering, busy mind and coping with the feelings that it throws at us. It's a full time job having an active mind, and it's easy to lose connection with the things that really matter to us. We are only on this planet for a short time. Identifying our values reconnects us with what we really think is important. Knowing what matters to us can help us decide how we are going to act in our everyday lives. "Living by your values" is the concept of ensuring that our **daily behaviours reflect what we really care about,** as opposed to living day to day at the mercy of our thoughts.

Our values are already there. It's simply a matter of uncovering what they are. Once we know what we stand for in our heart of hearts, it **gets easier to make decisions** based on something truly meaningful, and it's easier to go against old patterns of thinking that are familiar but not necessarily going to make us happy and fulfilled.

FINDING YOUR VALUES

Your 85th Birthday Party

Imagine that it's your 85th birthday. You are reaching the end of a long, and wonderful life. Imagine that you have reached this great age and have absolutely no regrets about how you have lived. As you reflect on your experiences, you realise that the reason you feel such **deep contentment with yourself and how you have lived** is because you are strongly connected with your gut: your sense of what is right and important to you. Like everyone, you've had to wrestle with negative thoughts, insecurities, fears, and doubts. But you've never allowed these overlearned patterns make your decisions for you – you've learned instead to attach yourself to your core values instead, and let them guide you.

Your family and friends are about to arrive for a grand birthday lunch.

At this lunch, you are going to give a speech. Your family, aware of your wisdom, have asked you to speak to them about how to live. They want to know what are the fundamental things that have guided you through life?

Your job is to write down what you'd love to tell them. This speech is not about what you may have achieved in your life, financially or professionally. This speech is about **who you are as a human being,** what kinds of principles and ideas guide you. What you stand for, what's truly important.

Take some time, and use the space opposite to write the kind of speech you'd love to give your family and friends. Remember this is an 'ideal' – don't write the speech that you think you might make, if you had to do it today. This is a fantasy speech, to get you connected to who you'd really love to be, the kinds of things you'd love in your innermost heart to stand for. Write away:

Here is my 85th birthday speech:

Thank you to my wonderful family and friends for coming today. I'm so deeply touched and feel so lucky to be surrounded by you all. You've asked me what is really important in life. I realise as I write this speech how much has changed as I grew older: when I was young I was convinced I knew everything, now I see that the certainty I had back then closed me off

from actually seeing. Through painful experience I have learned **the value of curiosity** rather than certainty. I have gained so much in my life by opening up and allowing myself to learn more. And I do love learning, and knowledge.

I also can't imagine being as contented as I am now if I hadn't connected with the **power of compassion, kindness and love.** These were not attributes that were taught to me in my early years, but I came to understand that they were deep within me, and learning to listen to this part truly transformed my life. For all of you who I love, I encourage you to use this compassion, love and kindness that is within, to guide you even if it seems scary.

Connection with others and to myself is key. This means staying in connection with my own thoughts and feelings. Knowing myself, and keeping connected with me even if I don't like what is going on for me! Having my own back even when I'm not behaving like my best self. Connecting with others is something I deeply value. Doing my best to **stay open with people and let them in,** and to use compassion to stay connected with what's happening for them. Feeling connected to others gives me a deep sense of peace and belonging.

Patience and honesty are deeply held values for me as well. **Slowing down and being mindful** helps me to connect back with patience, allowing things to be as they will and not hurrying everything up or trying to control everything. Being patient has enriched my life and allowed me to take pleasure in the details rather than rushing off to the end. Honesty: with myself, with others. So valuable. Sometimes painful, sometimes wonderful, but it's just a given. We can't get through life deceiving ourselves or others, living this way isn't satisfying. Being genuine and me and not being afraid of that being 'wrong'.

Finally, **laughing and seeing the fun in things** is important. Not taking myself too seriously and having a great big belly laugh at least once a day.

UNCOVERING YOUR VALUES

Once you have written your speech, grab a highlighter and go back through what you have written. Highlight the words that describe an attribute or value that you hold dearly.

When I do that, I come out with:

- curiosity
- opening up
- learning and knowledge
- compassionate
- kindness
- love
- connection with self and others
- patience
- honesty
- fun and laughter

Rather neatly, these are my 'top ten' values. Now I have a short list of words that describe what's actually important to me in my life.

You don't need to have 10 values – there is no 'right' number. Everybody is different, it doesn't matter if you only have a few, or if you have many. The most important thing to remember is that these are **genuine, heartfelt characteristics** that hit you in the 'gut' level.

Using Values In Your Everyday Life

Once you have an idea of your values, you can start using them to guide you, rather than relying on your overlearned thought patterns. A simple way to get started is to ask yourself:

What's my value here?

This question helps you to anchor yourself in a different direction – your values. Opposite are some examples of how using this question can change your life:

USING VALUES TO MAKE DECISIONS

Kelly came from a very poverty stricken childhood, and as a result she had many recurring fears about not having enough money. This fear was driving her to work overtime in a job she hated, even though she knew that she really wanted to study naturopathy. When she asked herself, 'what's my value here?', she was able to see that from a values perspective, studying was what she truly wanted to do, as she loved helping people and loved learning. The fear was holding her back. By choosing to connect with her value, Kelly was able to **move in a direction that she felt was right** for her, in spite of the fear.

USING VALUES TO OVERCOME THE MIND

Katie was struggling with her elderly mother, who was becoming increasingly demanding of her time. Katie had three children under the age of ten, and worked part-time. She was also very involved in her husband's start-up business, helping him to organise and plan various aspects of the new company's running. Katie was exhausted, and battling with chronic fatigue syndrome.

Katie's overlearned pattern of thinking and feeling revolved around themes of putting others needs before herself, not rocking the boat, and avoiding conflict. She suffered from a lot of inner judgement, which

Identifying our values reconnects us with what we really think is important.

worsened whenever Katie tried to be assertive with people around her.

Katie's 85th birthday exercise was hard for her, as she wrestled with the idea of people coming to celebrate her life. She realised she was uncomfortable with the thought of people actually listening to her point of view, something she'd never practised in her real life. By using compassionate mindfulness to **let these uncomfortable thoughts go,** she was able to connect with the speech she would love to give, and it surprised her greatly. Here is a part of her speech:

"The best advice I could give you on how to live to be as happy and satisfied as I am today is to look after yourself. For a long time I didn't, I tried to please everybody else, but I ended up very sick from that way of living. Thankfully I learned from that and now I know that my deep contentment with my life is because **I look after me.** When I really look after me, everything in my life is better, and even the relationships I have with people are better – more real, more equal."

So Katie learned that she deeply valued looking after herself. Once she was aware of this value, she was able to start using it, almost immediately, and it changed her life:

"My mother called with another demand. She wanted me to come over and change a light bulb for her. It was the end of another terrifically long day and I was exhausted. The chronic fatigue was really playing up and I felt like I could hardly move, but when she asked me I felt myself automatically sitting up and swinging my legs off the bed, about to grab the car keys. Then I remembered our conversation, and my 85th birthday, and how I wanted to live. I asked myself 'what's my value here?'. And I heard myself saying 'you need to look after yourself'.

Instead of just rushing over there, I told my mother that I was unwell, and wouldn't be able to make it over straight away. I offered to come tomorrow, when my day was quiet and I wouldn't have to rush. To my surprise my mother was ok about it! She even made a joke about dinner by candlelight. Ok so perhaps she wasn't joking, but I didn't let the guilt and the judgement thoughts get to me. I just reminded myself that **I don't have to be guided anymore by these reflexive ways of thinking.** I even found that my hand was on my heart when I was connecting with the value. It felt strangely peaceful to give myself permission to go with my value, and it's good to know that even though the judgemental thoughts still happened, I didn't have to do what it said anymore".

Katie continued to work on connecting with her values, and by putting up boundaries with other people, she found that she had a lot more time on her hands than she first imagined. She became less exhausted, and more fulfilled.

VALUES AREN'T ALWAYS EASY

Hayes, a leading researcher in the area of values, says "Values are... a chosen direction in which an individual can always move, no matter what milestones are reached." In other words, **values are the path which you would like to follow in your life.** Even if you find that you are off your path, you can always return – because the value is always there.

Imagine two pathways, winding their way through the forest. Both of them end up in the same place, but take different routes. One of these pathways is very wide and appears well trodden. This pathway is relatively flat and straight, with no twists and turns. The landscape around this pathway is pretty repetitive and there are no real surprises. The other pathway is less well worn. This path winds its way through the bush, with many twists and turns along the way. At times the path is uphill, at other times it is flat, and at other times it heads downhill. With such variation, the landscape around this path is **constantly changing.** The view from the path is sometimes panoramic, sometimes breathtakingly beautiful, and sometimes there is no view at all.

Choosing to live your life guided by values is like walking the second pathway. **It can at times be difficult.** This is because values can take effort. You may have to make an active choice to act in line with what you believe in. You may have to face up to difficult feelings, such as anxiety, or fear, or feeling uncomfortable. But these choices to face up to hardship are worth it for the wonderful, beautiful, fulfilling experiences they can give you. Values based living may not be the easiest path to take each day, but it is a path that **makes your life more vital and meaningful.**

Choosing the 'easy' path – i.e. choosing to live guided only by what feels more comfortable, familiar, or easy – may be something you have chosen to do until now. Is this really how you want to live your life?

FLEXIBILITY

When we talk about values, it is easy to make them a 'rule' to live by. Our human minds love to perfect, to improve and to strive. **But values are not rules.** They are ideals, and no-one can be ideal all of the time. I deeply value honesty, but in my life I am by no means honest all of the time!

The self-compassionate approach to mindful living is approaching everything with an **attitude of curiosity, and flexibility.** This means understanding that you're not always going to be perfect with your values, and that's ok. If you know that at the moment you're far away from what you value, try not to judge that. Simply notice that you are away from your value, in an objective, compassionate way. Do your best to take some small steps to get closer to your value, and resist the urge to change everything all at once.

VALUES IN CONFLICT

Sometimes you can be at war with your own values. In life, we can run into values dilemmas. For example, Paul came to therapy because he was conflicted about his relationship.

Paul suffered with bipolar disorder, and like many with this diagnosis, he didn't always want to take his medication. When he was in a manic state, Paul felt extremely creative and was able to paint and draw. However, when he was manic, Paul also became sexually promiscuous and compulsive with alcohol and drugs. This was having a terrible impact on his relationship with his wife, with whom he had just fathered a child.

Paul's values work revealed that he truly valued creativity and his artistic streak. He also valued monogamous love and trust with his partner. Paul found himself with a dilemma – when he was close to one value he put himself in conflict with another.

This was a very difficult time for Paul as he grappled with his **conflicting values.** He was able to hold all of this confusion by using mindfulness and self-compassion skills, which helped him avoid a further **trap of judgement and self-recrimination.**

Paul eventually decided that in the big scheme of his life, monogamous love and trust were more highly valued than creativity. He decided to take his medication, and spent some time sitting with the grief that this decision sparked. Paul and his wife were able to discuss his grief, and they together came up with some lovely creative solutions. Paul and his wife planned times in which he would not take his medications, and the family booked holidays in remote locations in outback Australia. Paul found that he was able to channel his creative streak into these short bursts of time, and without the distraction of other women or alcohol and drugs (there's no internet in the outback!), his artwork became even better.

Not all values conflicts are as dramatic as Pauls. But they can occur, and if they do, it's useful to **use self-compassion and mindfulness to help you work through it.** If you're really struggling, seeing a therapist who works with values can help you towards resolution.

SUMMARY

A very quick 'how to' use your values in your everyday life guide:
1. Make a list of your most important values and keep them somewhere you'll see them (on the fridge, in your phone, next to your bed, in your wallet)
2. In life, get in the habit of asking yourself "What's my value here?" when decisions pop up
3. If you find that you are away from your value, **don't beat yourself up.** Understand that it's impossible to be close to our values all of the time. Take it easy and slowly. Ask yourself, "What's a small step I can take towards my value today?"

ANCHORING

As you become more familiar with the concepts and practices in this book, there's a nice **'short cut'** that you can take to help you to manage yourself. Learning compassionate mindfulness is a wonderful skill which can help you to **see your thoughts and feelings without getting overly wrapped up in them.** The compassion focus helps you to stay non-judgemental and understanding towards yourself while you're noticing your thoughts and feelings.

Many of my clients start to realise that there are 'two parts' of themselves: the worried mind – full of racing thoughts, panic, extreme thoughts, strong negative feelings, and of course, judgement – and then there's a different part. This different part is what I consider to be the 'real' you – the compassionate mind, the wise mind. This part of you knows your values, is in connection with what's really important in your life, and is able to withstand the difficult thoughts and feelings that are part of every human being's life.

To start with, most of my clients live primarily in the 'worried mind'. This connection causes a lot of suffering. During therapy, clients learn the skill of compassionate mindfulness, and with a spirit of curiosity, non-judgement, and kindness, get to know their worried minds. We then turn to uncovering values, and to learning how to spend more time in the **'wise mind'**, or at least how to turn towards it when things get tough.

The concept of **'anchoring'** means getting to know where your attention or focus is. If you're not in a good place, it's likely that you are 'anchoring' your attention with the worried mind. If you notice this is happening, make an intention to 'pull out' of the worried mind and 're-anchor' in the wise mind.

Some ways of helping yourself do this might be:

◆ Who's talking here – worried mind or wise mind?
◆ Where is my focus?
◆ What does my wise mind think about this?
◆ How can I help myself connect to my wise mind?

BECOMING SOFTER

A lovely and simple way to put everything together when it comes to living a more compassionate and mindful life is the acronym **SOFTER.**

SOFTER breaks down in the following way:

Stop: take a moment to pause, and come into the moment. Stop whatever you are doing and simply be.

Observe: take the perspective of the sun, gently pulling out of your tree and noticing your

Feelings and Thoughts: what is your mind saying? How is this self-talk making you feel? What emotions are popping up?

Embrace: yourself for this experience, framing it as pain or struggle. Be kind towards yourself in this moment rather than judgemental. This involves being very accepting of your painful thoughts and feelings, being kind to yourself as it is happening, and remembering that all of this is part of being human.

Return: to your wise mind, to your values, to help you to decide what to do.

Once I have taught clients the essential skills of compassionate mindfulness, the acronym SOFTER becomes their very quick, go-to guide of how to use the skills in everyday life. I use it myself, and find it helps in so many different situations.

SPREADING THE LOVE

We have spent a lot of time in this book discussing ways to increase your self-compassion. But self-compassion extends beyond improving our relationship with ourselves: it involves **building a kinder, more compassionate way of relating to other people** and to the world. As we have seen, a fundamental concept in self-compassion is the connection with common humanity: the idea that we are all human, all imperfect, and all connected in suffering.

There are many simple acts of kindness, connection, and generosity that you can try to build this idea of compassion into your life. This might be something very small, like deciding to smile at a stranger in the street, or to give up your seat on the bus for another person. To be kind to the tired mother on the plane with the crying baby rather than expressing impatience.

You could experiment with **random acts of kindness,** like paying for someone else's coffee at a cafe. You could make a sandwich for a homeless person. You could play with what Dorothy, a lovely client of mine, calls 'bespoke acts of kindness' – deliberate acts directed towards someone special in your life. In Dorothy's case, she made a beautiful birthday cake for her special nephew.

On a slightly bigger level, you could consider if there is something you could incorporate into your life that might foster this idea of kindness and connection. This might mean taking some of your possessions to a charity shop, or finding a way of volunteering your services to a cause you are passionate about. Whatever it is that might make you **feel more connected to this society you live in**. The idea is to connect, rather than to disconnect. To lean in to the idea of being human, to give, to open your heart rather than to close it up.

GRATITUDE PRACTICE

Our threat related minds don't automatically consider all that we have to be grateful for. And yet, focusing our attention on those parts of our life that are fulfilling, meaningful, and joyful has the potential to bring a lot of meaning to our lives.

A daily **gratitude practice** is a useful way of developing connection to that which is good. A question to ask which might help us to access gratitude are:

What am I grateful for today?

Some days, the answer will be apparent, on others, it might seem impossible to be grateful. And yet, even on the darkest of days, we can be grateful for having survived it.

When I try this, I'm amazed by **how much there is to be grateful for:** my noisy adorable children, my comfortable bed, my amazing clients, the sunshine, the smell of a gardenia, my morning coffee, a crunchy apple, a funny joke....Nothing huge has to happen in order for me to focus on gratitude. And this focus rubs off: the worried, negative mind still operates, but there is a rich and fulfilling alternative place for me to **anchor my attention** with: the self-compassionate, loving, kind fun mind that I have grown.

The idea is to connect, rather than to disconnect.

LOVING KINDNESS

A final, lovely gift for you is this beautiful meditation practice called loving kindness.

This meditation is frequently used in self-compassion practice as a way of building up the compassionate mind. It helps you to build up a habit of **seeing things from a calmer, more accepting position.** Research has found that loving-kindness meditation may be one of the most powerful ways to develop and grow self-compassion. Even just a few minutes of loving-kindness meditation relaxes your body and increases positive feelings and feelings of social connection.

I have found that the more I practice it, the easier it is for me to step into a more compassionate perspective in my everyday life, even when circumstances happen to challenge that intent.

Loving Kindness practice starts with a focus on the quality of compassion towards yourself and then extends this quality out towards others. It will leave you feeling peaceful, calm, and loving. I think it's a great gift to give yourself at the end of a hard day.

Feel free to record yourself reading this script (using your phone), and then play it back to yourself. If you would prefer to hear my voice guiding you through this meditation, you can download it on itunes using this link: http://itunes.apple.com/album/id1035680975?ls=1&app=itunes

Loving Kindness Mediation
Making sure that you are sitting or lying down in a comfortable position. Taking some time now to gently close your eyes, and focus on your breath in and breathe out. All of your attention and focus is on how your lungs feel as they draw the breath in, and then let it go. Don't try to change how you are breathing, simply being with

each breath with an attitude of kind awareness.

Now casting your attention towards someone in your life towards whom you have **bottomless love.** This might be someone you know right now, or someone from the past. It can even be a beloved pet. Whatever you call up, whatever comes to mind, ensure that they are associated in your heart with deep love and affection.

Bring up this person clearly in your minds' eye, and allow yourself to feel all of the positive loving emotions that naturally occur. Observe, notice, and immerse yourself in these emotions. This is compassion.

Now, letting this person fade from your awareness, but keeping hold of the feelings of love and compassion that have arisen within you.

Now call yourself up in your minds' eye. Allowing your focus to be on yourself. And holding these loving feelings closely, let the following words become your words:

May I be safe.
May I be happy.
May I be healthy.
May I live with ease.

Now call into your minds' eye somebody in your life who has always been there for you. Someone who has been a **loving support** to you during your life. Somebody you respect. And sending to them these words:

May you be safe.
May you be happy.

May you be healthy.
May you live with ease.

And now calling to mind a person who you may not know... someone in your community who you see but perhaps don't speak with... a neighbour...someone on the bus..... and send to them these words:

May you be safe.
May you be happy.
May you be healthy.
May you live with ease.

And now switch your attention towards someone in your life who has irritated you recently. Someone who has brought to you some difficult feelings...someone you have struggled with. And to them, send them these words:

May you be safe.
May you be happy.
May you be healthy.
May you live with ease.

And now, imagining that you could call to mind your community, of which you are part. Your family, your friends, your acquaintances...and even more broadly to the people in your town or city...the country, and even further. Out towards **all of humanity.** To them send these words:

May we be safe.
May we be happy.
May we be healthy.
May we live with ease.

And allowing yourself to sit with these feelings and intentions of loving kindness.

Bringing you awareness now back to your breath as it enters and leaves your body. In a few minutes, when you feel ready, open your eyes and return to your day, bringing an attitude of loving kindness to all that you do.

How Was That For You?

Generally people find this meditation to be very pleasant indeed. It's lovely to focus on **sharing the idea of compassion** with other people, near and far.

Some of my clients feel a little cynical about starting this kind of practice, especially if their minds are particularly judgemental. It's ok to have a defensive response. This type of kindness is very different, and it can make us feel vulnerable. If you are struggling, simply accept that it's hard for your mind to deal with, and do your best to keep a compassionate attitude towards **your own struggle.** And of course, don't be afraid to see a therapist for help with it if it's too much to do on your own!

Bringing Loving-Kindness Into Your Everyday Life

It is possible to extend and grow and attitude of compassion into your world. In addition to regular loving-kindness meditation, you can take the opportunity during the day to simply remind yourself:

May I be safe.
May I be happy.
May I be healthy.
May I live with ease.

Or, you can send it quietly to somebody else:

May you be safe.
May you be happy.
May you be healthy.
May you live with ease.

30 DAYS OF KINDFULNESS

I hope that this book has helped you to understand more about compassionate mindfulness, about your own thinking mind, and how to **connect with your wise mind**. I hope that you've practised some of the exercises and meditations as you've been reading the book, and that they have helped you in some way or another.

It can seem a little overwhelming to think of how to put all of this knowledge into practice in your everyday life, especially if you're a busy person with lots on your plate already.

This is why I have put together for you a very simple 30 day plan to get you started. Please think of this not as a 'mindfulness challenge', or something that you have to rigidly 'get right'. I prefer to think of it as **an invitation to treat yourself well**. Or as an opportunity to give yourself a lovely gift each day for 30 days. And if on some of those days you don't feel like doing it, that's ok as well. Just be gentle with yourself, and see what happens.

Research has shown that just a few minutes of compassionate mindfulness practice can have **benefits on our stress levels** and feelings of connection to other people. Regular practice can actually change how our brains operate. It's totally up to you how much or how little you can do. Any small change is worth it.

The 30 days have been carefully structured. Each day you'll start by **connecting with yourself** and with a loving intention for the day. And at the end of each day, you'll be invited to spend a minute or so focusing on something that you've been grateful for that day. Each of these practices should take only a minute or so of your time, and doing it brings a lovely framework to each day.

In between the morning and evening practices, you'll be given a unique compassionate mindfulness activity that will require your focus for no longer than a few minutes. Firstly, the focus is on the basics of **awareness and coming into the present moment**. We then add awareness of your thoughts and feelings, and practice being kind towards them. We then turn towards anchoring in the wise mind, letting this part of ourselves make decisions. And lastly, we turn towards **loving kindness**, which helps us to strengthen our compassionate mind and connect us in a very meaningful way to other people and the world. Does this sound complicated? I hope not – I've made it as uncomplicated as I can. You are of course welcome to do much more mindfulness practice during your day, and enjoy the added richness that it can give you.

So above all, enjoy the gift of compassionate mindfulness.

Day	Upon waking	5 minute dips	Last Thing Before Sleep
1	Hand on your heart as soon as you are awake. Feeling the warmth of your hand on your chest. Sending yourself best wishes for the day ahead. May I be safe. May I be happy. May I be healthy. I wish myself peace.	Pause at some point in your day and be in that moment. "Here....now" do this just once, or a few times, whatever suits you	What am I grateful for today? Hand on heart. You can write it down or just call it up in your thoughts.
2	Hand on your heart as soon as you are awake. Feeling the warmth of your hand on your chest. Sending yourself best wishes for the day ahead. May I be safe. May I be happy. May I be healthy. I wish myself peace.	Today, play with just sitting. Give yourself permission to sit for 2 minutes between tasks. In those 2 minutes, simply be with sitting. "Here...now...sitting" do this just once, or a few times, whatever suits you	What am I grateful for today? Hand on heart. You can write it down or just call it up in your thoughts.
3	Hand on your heart as soon as you are awake. Feeling the warmth of your hand on your chest. Sending yourself best wishes for the day ahead. May I be safe. May I be happy. May I be healthy. I wish myself peace.	Today, play with pausing. Pause between tasks you'd ordinarily rush through, such a between putting on your first and second shoe or sock. Let your attention be with that pause. "Here...now...pausing. Noticing my feet". do this just once, or a few times, whatever suits you	What am I grateful for today? Hand on heart. You can write it down or just call it up in your thoughts.
4	Hand on your heart as soon as you are awake. Feeling the warmth of your hand on your chest. Sending yourself best wishes for the day ahead. May I be safe. May I be happy. May I be healthy. I wish myself peace.	Today, play with being present in the moment. At some point in your day check in. ask yourself "What's happening right now?" After you do this, remind yourself "Just this moment." do this just once, or a few times, whatever suits you	What am I grateful for today? Hand on heart. You can write it down or just call it up in your thoughts.

Day	Upon waking	5 minute dips	Last Thing Before Sleep
5	Hand on your heart as soon as you are awake. Feeling the warmth of your hand on your chest. Sending yourself best wishes for the day ahead. May I be safe. May I be happy. May I be healthy. I wish myself peace.	Today, play with being present in the moment. At some point in your day check in. ask yourself "What's happening right now?" After you do this, remind yourself "Just this moment. do this just once, or a few times, whatever suits you	What am I grateful for today? Hand on heart. You can write it down or just call it up in your thoughts.
6	Hand on your heart as soon as you are awake. Feeling the warmth of your hand on your chest. Sending yourself best wishes for the day ahead. May I be safe. May I be happy. May I be healthy. I wish myself peace.	Today, put your focus onto your breath. Dip into affectionate breathing. At some point, be with your breath "Kindness in, kindness out" do this just once, or a few times, whatever suits you	What am I grateful for today? Hand on heart. You can write it down or just call it up in your thoughts.
7	Hand on your heart as soon as you are awake. Feeling the warmth of your hand on your chest. Sending yourself best wishes for the day ahead. May I be safe. May I be happy. May I be healthy. I wish myself peace.	Play again with coming into affectionate breathing, using your shortcut 'kindness in, kindness out'. Pair this with either a half smile or a touch on your heart. do this just once, or a few times, whatever suits you	What am I grateful for today? Hand on heart. You can write it down or just call it up in your thoughts.
8	Hand on your heart as soon as you are awake. Feeling the warmth of your hand on your chest. Sending yourself best wishes for the day ahead. May I be safe. May I be happy. May I be healthy. I wish myself peace.	Play again with coming into affectionate breathing, using your shortcut 'kindness in, kindness out'. Pair this with either a half smile or a touch on your heart. do this just once, or a few times, whatever suits you	What am I grateful for today? Hand on heart. You can write it down or just call it up in your thoughts.

Day	Upon waking	5 minute dips	Last Thing Before Sleep
9	Hand on your heart as soon as you are awake. Feeling the warmth of your hand on your chest. Sending yourself best wishes for the day ahead. May I be safe. May I be happy. May I be healthy. I wish myself peace.	Play with your favourite sense and practice paying attention to it at various times in your day. If it's smell, ask yourself 'what can I smell right now?'	What am I grateful for today? Hand on heart. You can write it down or just call it up in your thoughts.
10	Hand on your heart as soon as you are awake. Feeling the warmth of your hand on your chest. Sending yourself best wishes for the day ahead. May I be safe. May I be happy. May I be healthy. I wish myself peace.	Play with connecting to your body today. Check in with it 'how is my body feeling right now?' Notice how it is feeling, and send thanks to your body for holding you do this just once, or a few times, whatever suits you	What am I grateful for today? Hand on heart. You can write it down or just call it up in your thoughts.
11	Hand on your heart as soon as you are awake. Feeling the warmth of your hand on your chest. Sending yourself best wishes for the day ahead. May I be safe. May I be happy. May I be healthy. I wish myself peace.	Do something boring mindfully: pick a boring task and pay full attention to it do this just once, or a few times, whatever suits you	What am I grateful for today? Hand on heart. You can write it down or just call it up in your thoughts.
12	Hand on your heart as soon as you are awake. Feeling the warmth of your hand on your chest. Sending yourself best wishes for the day ahead. May I be safe. May I be happy. May I be healthy. I wish myself peace.	Do something boring mindfully: pick a boring task and pay full attention to it do this just once, or a few times, whatever suits you	What am I grateful for today? Hand on heart. You can write it down or just call it up in your thoughts.
13	Hand on your heart as soon as you are awake. Feeling the warmth of your hand on your chest. Sending yourself best wishes for the day ahead. May I be safe. May I be happy. May I be healthy. I wish myself peace.	Today, dip into mindful eating. If you don't have time for a full mindful meal, enjoy some mindful bites. Delicious! do this just once, or a few times, whatever suits you	What am I grateful for today? Hand on heart. You can write it down or just call it up in your thoughts.

Day	Upon waking	5 minute dips	Last Thing Before Sleep
14	Hand on your heart as soon as you are awake. Feeling the warmth of your hand on your chest. Sending yourself best wishes for the day ahead. May I be safe. May I be happy. May I be healthy. I wish myself peace.	Today, go for a mindful walk. Allow your attention to be fully in your senses. do this just once, or a few times, whatever suits you	What am I grateful for today? Hand on heart. You can write it down or just call it up in your thoughts.
15	Hand on your heart as soon as you are awake. Feeling the warmth of your hand on your chest. Sending yourself best wishes for the day ahead. May I be safe. May I be happy. May I be healthy. I wish myself peace.	Today, practice connecting to your thinking mind. At some point today, step into the sun and notice what is happening in your thoughts, with a kind, objective attitude. "my mind is saying that..." "here's what my mind is saying..." "thanks mind...." do this just once, or a few times, whatever suits you	What am I grateful for today? Hand on heart. You can write it down or just call it up in your thoughts.
16	Hand on your heart as soon as you are awake. Feeling the warmth of your hand on your chest. Sending yourself best wishes for the day ahead. May I be safe. May I be happy. May I be healthy. I wish myself peace.	Today, practice 'putting it onto a leaf' and letting go of thoughts do this just once, or a few times, whatever suits you	What am I grateful for today? Hand on heart. You can write it down or just call it up in your thoughts.
17	Hand on your heart as soon as you are awake. Feeling the warmth of your hand on your chest. Sending yourself best wishes for the day ahead. May I be safe. May I be happy. May I be healthy. I wish myself peace.	Today, practice 'putting it onto a leaf' and letting go of thoughts do this just once, or a few times, whatever suits you	What am I grateful for today? Hand on heart. You can write it down or just call it up in your thoughts.

Day	Upon waking	5 minute dips	Last Thing Before Sleep
18	Hand on your heart as soon as you are awake. Feeling the warmth of your hand on your chest. Sending yourself best wishes for the day ahead. May I be safe. May I be happy. May I be healthy. I wish myself peace.	Today, practice noticing, accepting, and looking after your feelings do this just once, or a few times, whatever suits you	What am I grateful for today? Hand on heart. You can write it down or just call it up in your thoughts.
19	Hand on your heart as soon as you are awake. Feeling the warmth of your hand on your chest. Sending yourself best wishes for the day ahead. May I be safe. May I be happy. May I be healthy. I wish myself peace.	Today, practice noticing, accepting, and looking after your feelings do this just once, or a few times, whatever suits you	What am I grateful for today? Hand on heart. You can write it down or just call it up in your thoughts.
20	Hand on your heart as soon as you are awake. Feeling the warmth of your hand on your chest. Sending yourself best wishes for the day ahead. May I be safe. May I be happy. May I be healthy. I wish myself peace.	Today, try your best to look after both your thoughts and feelings from the perspective of the sun. Observe, accept everything that's going on, with a spirit of kindness towards yourself	What am I grateful for today? Hand on heart. You can write it down or just call it up in your thoughts.
21	Hand on your heart as soon as you are awake. Feeling the warmth of your hand on your chest. Sending yourself best wishes for the day ahead. May I be safe. May I be happy. May I be healthy. I wish myself peace.	Today, if you notice you are struggling with something, ask yourself "what would I say to a dear friend who I loved if they were going through this?"	What am I grateful for today? Hand on heart. You can write it down or just call it up in your thoughts.

Day	Upon waking	5 minute dips	Last Thing Before Sleep
22	Hand on your heart as soon as you are awake. Feeling the warmth of your hand on your chest. Sending yourself best wishes for the day ahead. May I be safe. May I be happy. May I be healthy. I wish myself peace.	Today, if you notice you are struggling with something, ask yourself "what would I say to a dear friend who I loved if they were going through this?" afterwards, ask yourself "what would be good for me to do right now? "what do I really need in this moment?"	What am I grateful for today? Hand on heart. You can write it down or just call it up in your thoughts.
23	Hand on your heart as soon as you are awake. Feeling the warmth of your hand on your chest. Sending yourself best wishes for the day ahead. May I be safe. May I be happy. May I be healthy. I wish myself peace.	Today, if you notice you are struggling with something, ask yourself "what would I say to a dear friend who I loved if they were going through this?" afterwards, ask yourself "what would be good for me to do right now? "what do I really need in this moment?"	What am I grateful for today? Hand on heart. You can write it down or just call it up in your thoughts.
24	Hand on your heart as soon as you are awake. Feeling the warmth of your hand on your chest. Sending yourself best wishes for the day ahead. May I be safe. May I be happy. May I be healthy. I wish myself peace.	Today at some point, think of your sweet spot and connect with joy	What am I grateful for today? Hand on heart. You can write it down or just call it up in your thoughts.
25	Hand on your heart as soon as you are awake. Feeling the warmth of your hand on your chest. Sending yourself best wishes for the day ahead. May I be safe. May I be happy. May I be healthy. I wish myself peace.	Today at some point, connect with the acronym SOFTER...see what shows up	What am I grateful for today? Hand on heart. You can write it down or just call it up in your thoughts.

Day	Upon waking	5 minute dips	Last Thing Before Sleep
26	Hand on your heart as soon as you are awake. Feeling the warmth of your hand on your chest. Sending yourself best wishes for the day ahead. May I be safe. May I be happy. May I be healthy. I wish myself peace.	Today at some point, connect with the acronym SOFTER...see what shows up	What am I grateful for today? Hand on heart. You can write it down or just call it up in your thoughts.
27	Hand on your heart as soon as you are awake. Feeling the warmth of your hand on your chest. Sending yourself best wishes for the day ahead. May I be safe. May I be happy. May I be healthy. I wish myself peace.	Today at some point, connect with the acronym SOFTER...see what shows up	What am I grateful for today? Hand on heart. You can write it down or just call it up in your thoughts.
28	Hand on your heart as soon as you are awake. Feeling the warmth of your hand on your chest. Sending yourself best wishes for the day ahead. May I be safe. May I be happy. May I be healthy. I wish myself peace.	Today at some point, connect with the acronym SOFTER...see what shows up	What am I grateful for today? Hand on heart. You can write it down or just call it up in your thoughts.
29	Hand on your heart as soon as you are awake. Feeling the warmth of your hand on your chest. Sending yourself best wishes for the day ahead. May I be safe. May I be happy. May I be healthy. I wish myself peace.	Today, take yourself out for a special occasion. Buy yourself a lovely bunch of flowers, or have a really nice lunch. Treat yourself	What am I grateful for today? Hand on heart. You can write it down or just call it up in your thoughts.
30	Hand on your heart as soon as you are awake. Feeling the warmth of your hand on your chest. Sending yourself best wishes for the day ahead. May I be safe. May I be happy. May I be healthy. I wish myself peace.	Today, do a random or bespoke act of kindness for someone else	What am I grateful for today? Hand on heart. You can write it down or just call it up in your thoughts.

STAYING CONNECTED

I would really love to hear from you and to hear how you're going with the 30 days. Please feel free to connect with me. My websites are www.self.net.au and www.treatyourselfwell.com.au. If you'd like to email, send to essentials@self.net.au. I'm on twitter at @LouiseAdamstyw, and you can also 'like' my Facebook page, Treat Yourself Well Sydney, which is a great place to learn about what I'm doing and to post your thoughts about the book and the practice of self-compassion. Thank you so much for taking the time to read this book. Take care of yourself!

INDEX